inside and out,
vel."

zer Prize winner and
Is How You Lose Her

, and tools to help
the modern-day woman find her soul mate without
wasting her valuable time and precious resources on
the wrong men."

—DR. JENN BERMAN, host of
VH1's *Couples Therapy* and *The Love and Sex Show
with Dr. Jenn* on Cosmo Radio, Sirius XM

"From my first conversation with Dr. Walsh, I knew
she was the real deal: caring, patient, knowledgeable.
This book comes from the place that makes her so
special—the HEART."

—DON LEMON, host of *CNN Newsroom*

"Dr. Walsh brings tremendous insight and intelligence
to the mysteries of the modern game of mating. You
will come away wiser and smarter. It's the best book
I've read this year."

—DAVID M. BUSS, author of
The Evolution of Desire: Strategies of Human Mating

"Dr. Walsh takes readers on a frank and valuable tour
of how the 'mating market' has changed—and how
you can improve your odds of finding lasting love."

—MARK REGNERUS, coauthor of
*Premarital Sex in America: How Young Americans Meet,
Mate, and Think About Marrying*

"*The 30-Day Love Detox* is like a GPS to help you
navigate the changing com   der roles,
dating, marriage, relations
mitment in postmodern A
doesn't make you think,

Department of Sociology,

the 30-day love detox

Cleanse Yourself of Bad Boys, Cheaters, and Men Who Won't Commit— And Find a Real Relationship

DR. WENDY WALSH

RODALE.

Sex and Values at Rodale

We believe that an active and healthy sex life, based on mutual consent and respect between partners, is an important component of physical and mental well-being. We also respect that sex is a private matter and that each person has a different opinion of what sexual practices or levels of discourse are appropriate. Rodale is committed to offering responsible, practical advice about sexual matters, supported by accredited professionals and legitimate scientific research. Our goal—for sex and all other topics—is to publish information that empowers people's lives.

Mention of specific companies, organizations, or authorities in this book does not imply endorsement by the author or publisher, nor does mention of specific companies, organizations, or authorities imply that they endorse this book, its author, or the publisher.

Internet addresses and telephone numbers given in this book were accurate at the time it went to press.

Rodale books may be purchased for business or promotional use or for special sales. For information, please write to:

Special Markets Department, Rodale Inc., 733 Third Avenue, New York, NY 10017

Printed in the United States of America

Rodale Inc. makes every effort to use acid-free ♾, recycled paper ♻.

The Sexual Relationships Questionnaire in Chapter 3 is used with permission from Omri Gillath, PhD.

Understanding Your Gender Style in Chapter 3 is adapted from the Dual-Career Family Scale with permission from Brian Pendleton, PhD.

Book design by Mike Smith

Library of Congress Cataloging-in-Publication Data is on file with the publisher.

ISBN 978–1–60961–970-1 paperback

Distributed to the trade by Macmillan

2   4   6   8   10   9   7   5   3   1   paperback

RODALE.

We inspire and enable people to improve their lives and the world around them.

rodalebooks.com

To my grandmother, Agnes.
Her farm-wife wisdom about men
still rings true: "Have them wash up
before you feed them."

Contents

Acknowledgments

*W*ho says books are a dying art? Not the dozens of people who helped bring my ideas to life!

I have to start with my tireless, energetic, and whip-smart agent, Lacy Lynch, and the loyal team at Dupree Miller & Associates in Dallas. Jan Miller and Shannon Marven, I am indebted to you. And that happy Texas gal who answers the phones. I call your offices sometimes just to get cheered up.

Then there is my bright, risk-taking editor, Ursula Cary, who wasn't scared off by my message that runs contrary to our culture. Her wise eyes on my sometimes rambling text helped me steer the ship straight. Couldn't have done it without you. Thanks also to Hope Clarke, Elizabeth Neal, Mike Smith, Danielle Lynn, Brent Gallenberger, and the rest of the team at Rodale Inc.

And to my other hero, my research assistant, Lauren Jensen, who didn't let her graduate degree stop her from pitching in with my kids if that's what it took to get this book done. Your attention to detail (no, I didn't call you anal!) was exactly what my reference section needed and what I lack. Thanks, Lauren.

Back when I wrote for television news, a producer friend told me I had a unique talent for taking complicated scientific material and turning it into words that everyone could understand. I don't dumb ideas down. I try to make them accessible. But my talent would be useless if I were not gifted with access to some of the most brilliant minds doing often-unchampioned research behind the hallowed gates of university labs. I was thrilled and awed that so many of you took the time to take my calls and answer my e-mails to help me better understand the current state of sex and love. Thanks to David Buss, PhD; Brian Pendleton, PhD; Mark Regnerus, PhD; Omri Gillath, PhD; Sandra Metts, PhD; Anthony Paik, PhD; Dean Busby, PhD; Meg Jay, PhD; Juliet Richters, PhD; and Joan Williams, JD, of UC Hastings Law School.

I would be remiss if I didn't mention Dr. Kevin Volkan, my mentor at California State University, Channel Islands. Chatting with you always makes me feel smarter. And to all the passionate students at CSUCI who offered anecdotes and insight into today's dating market, I am grateful. And thanks to the many women who attended my wine and cheese focus groups. Your brave personal stories really helped me apply the science to real-world experiences.

Outside of the book world, I have a team that helps me in all aspects of my brand, from television and public speaking to online partnerships: Melissa Van Fleet at Ken Lindner & Associates, David McGriff at Stroock & Stroock & Levan, Brittany Sykes at Teszler P.R., Toby Sembower and Hayley Mathis at DatingAdvice.com, Jon Kroll at Popsicle Pictures, and Henry Schleiff at Investigation Discovery Network. Thank you all for your support.

To all my friends at CNN and HLN, but especially those with whom I've worked so closely at the CNN newsroom: Jenny Cook, Richard Wybrow, Andreas Preuss, Tina Kim, and, of course, the anchor I would marry if I could, the brilliant, kind, and funny Don Lemon. I am so blessed to have all of you in my life.

And my thanks to Dr. Phil and the entire executive team at *The Doctors*. I am deeply grateful to Carla Pennington, Jay McGraw, and Andrew Scher.

Finally, to my daughters, Carrington and Jones, every day you bring me great joy and peace that can only come from healthy attachments. When you finally fly from my nest, I will hold you with my heart forever. This is one love relationship that will never break up.

Introduction

I won't lie. I have a relationship hangover. It's the hangover many women experience after watching endless *Sex and the City* reruns and movies. The lives of those fabulous women and their New York adventures are deliciously addictive but can leave you with a serious headache—and heartache. The reality is very different. The true story of single women can often feel more like a tragedy than a lighthearted romp. None of my girlfriends ended up marrying Mr. Big. None of us has the genes or moxie to vamp like Samantha. None is in a storybook family like Charlotte. And no one can afford that wardrobe!

Instead, two of my friends got the human papillomavirus and cancer that led to hysterectomies before they were able to meet a man and settle down. One friend dated a commitment phobe who strung her along for years before she got him to marry her one weekend in Vegas. He then dangled the idea of having a baby in front of her for another decade until her fertility window slammed shut. She's divorced now, raising a dog. And plenty of other friends are struggling single mothers.

But this doesn't have to be you! You were born at the most perfect time in female human history—a time of unprecedented freedom and power and a time of exploding research on sexuality and human attachment. The women before you fumbled around in the dark for dating rules and came up with mixed messages: Be free but not too free. Play hard to get and go after what you want. Keep him close by not letting him know you want a commitment. But these rules just help you play a game; they don't enable you to find the wonderfully fulfilling, committed relationship you deserve. In this book, I'll tell you the truth about love, sex, courtship, and commitment.

This book is for you no matter what your mind-set on love and marriage. You might be a progressive gal who is having fun enjoying your sexuality but wants kids in a few years, or maybe you wait to have sex until you see if he's marriage material. You could be the modern girl who doesn't believe in marriage and is unsure about kids but still gets confused when fun guys scram after great sex. Or maybe you believe in marriage and are totally frustrated by serial dating that seems to lead nowhere. This book is also for you if you have a boyfriend and don't know how to ask for sexual exclusivity or relationship definition. Maybe you have invested a couple of years in a dude—or are even living together—while he's shirking conversations about the future. No matter your situation, the research in this book will make you very clear about who you are, what kind of relationship is best for you, and how to get your needs met.

In this book, I'm going to ask you to do a couple of difficult things. I'm going to ask you to purge junk food men who are eating up your time and giving you pretend power. (Don't worry, I'll also give you some strategies to remedy male withdrawal syndrome.) And I'm going to ask you to delay the onset of sex for at least thirty days when you meet a new guy. Please understand that this is not some old-fashioned gimmick to manipulate men. This is designed to get sex hormones out of the way while you two make some intelligent choices. And I'll tell you how women all over the world succeed in love. The clear step-by-step five-part attachment strategy is based in solid scientific research and, if followed correctly, can help you create the kind of relationship that is perfectly suited to you. I'll also introduce you to the powerful cavewoman who lives inside of you and whose ancient wisdom has helped you get here in the first place. I met my own cavewoman when I gave birth to babies, but you'll meet your enormous power much earlier.

I used to think of myself as the Carrie Bradshaw type, enjoying my fun-filled twenties and early thirties, making a living writing books called *The Boyfriend Test* and *The Girlfriend Test,* and championing women's sexual freedom. And then, at age 35, I had the good sense to check my inner clock at midnight on New Year's Eve and made a resolution: I wanted to have a family. But I needed to find a man first. And I did, quickly, find one encased in the body of a Greek god: He was gorgeous, successful, and smart. We moved in together and had two kids: I gave birth at ages 36 and 41.

But soon after we became a family of four, things fell apart. I didn't have the time or the tools to develop a proper relationship life plan, to understand my own needs and make sure he and I truly wanted the same things. My so-called Greek god slipped out under the wire. In an ironic twist, I had to sell almost every remnant from my single glory days on eBay—including designer bags, shoes, jewelry—so I could maintain a breastfeeding lifestyle without a male provider.

Despite my twists of fate, I still feel lucky. Of all the women I ran with in my twenties and early thirties, I'm the only one who was fortunate enough to become a mother. I love my kids so much. And I'm blessed to have a close circle of accidental "aunties" who pitch in, help out, and are huge contributors in my kids' lives.

I'm offering up this stark truth so a new generation of women can learn from it. My generation is in some ways a lost generation of women who were sold a false bill of goods about fertility, motherhood, and female sexual freedom. This doesn't have to be you. *The 30-Day Love Detox* will help you avoid the pitfalls of sexual freedom: men who won't commit, hookups that lead nowhere, years of dating Mr. Wrong, or even a missed fertility window.

I admit that for some young women today, things are even more complicated and confusing. Dating is no longer a place where men and women understand certain rituals. While it once was liberating for women to break all the rules, it has created an environment in which men no longer feel they need to use courtship to obtain sex. As I will describe in this book, a high-supply sexual economy can be dangerous, unchartered waters for many women. We've lost important rituals that gave us valuable information about a man's intentions. In this information vacuum, too many women are deluded into thinking that a sexual hookup is a ticket in a potential husband lottery.

One sexuality researcher I spoke with apologized for sounding conservative when he told me that separating babies from sex and sex from marriage has made men a whole lot happier than women. His apology is why *The 30-Day Love Detox* is so unique. This book's message about slow love doesn't come from a place of political conservatism or religion. It comes from hard science and sound sociological research. It's not a lecture about morals or traditional gender roles but is a thinking woman's tool. This book is your ticket to a healthy relationship.

The 30-Day Love Detox is the antidote to an increasingly vapid hookup culture.

If you have trouble meeting men, this book isn't for you. If you have trouble meeting like-minded, commitment-oriented men who share your vision of a future, then this book is exactly the medicine you need. I'm here to tell you that you have the power to control your love life! And in this time of relationship "freedom," you can choose to have any number of meaningful attachments. You can have a boyfriend or a stay-over relationship or you can cohabit. And if you still want a traditional marriage, right down to rings, flowers, and self-written vows, you have a right to that too. But each of these kinds of relationships has a specific set of risks and rewards I'll tell you about so you can make your relationship plans very carefully.

These are your rights as a woman. But unlike your civil rights, they won't be handed to you in a decree and no court of law will enforce them. You have to go out and earn the right to partner with a good man, and the only person who will protect your rights is you. And I promise to tell you exactly how to do that with *The 30-Day Love Detox*.

To get a picture of what you're up against, I want you to imagine yourself as a well-tuned race car. You're sleek, fast, and powerful. Best of all, you can keep up with a male race car that's twice your size. So, you do. Speeding around the track of life, you're intoxicated with your own power. It's so much fun to tap bumpers with all the brawny machines on the track, knowing they all want to race with you. But suddenly, the unthinkable happens. Your car slams into a wall that signals your race is over. The dude you're sparring with throws you a grin as he continues down his track and a newer model female car slides up beside him. Ladies, you may not know it, but you're in a race between the hookup track (which has no finish line for men) and your own fertility window. And your genes and heart are on the line.

In *The 30-Day Love Detox,* I'll explain our culture's current overproduction of sex and our underproduction of healthy families. I'll explain how the rise of women's economic power caused sex to rise in supply in our culture.

Then, I'll give you a wincingly honest account of how men react to a high-supply sexual economy: with fewer marriages, with less sexual commitment, and with smaller, uh, paychecks. It's true.

I'll also explain how female-to-female competition for men has wildly increased with the advent of cougars, MILFs, and sexpots all vying for a select group of marriageable men. In 1950, 72 percent of adults were married. Today, only half of adults are married. And the population of men who will participate in slow courtship that leads to commitment is shrinking each year. The first part of *The 30-Day Love Detox* will give you a stone-cold look at today's mating market and an eye-opening awareness of the biological and anthropological forces that shape your single status.

Then, I'll give you the good news. Great men who have the capacity to be monogamous and be involved with their families haven't become extinct! They may only be a little harder to see when they're lost in a sea of texts, e-mails, tweets, and Facebook friends. But I know exactly the strategies you need to clearly spot a commitment-oriented man. And here's more good news: Research has shown there are specific mating strategies used by women around the globe that help them discern the good guys from the bad boys—the "dads" from the "cads." If you think the mating game is won by "getting" one man to commit, you're dead wrong. The mating game is won by saying "Yes" to a select kind of man.

How do I know all this? Besides my "Carrie Bradshaw" experience, I have a PhD in clinical psychology with a specialty in human attachment. I lecture on human mating strategies at California State University at Channel Islands. As a clinician, I've counseled hundreds of singles and couples about their love lives. And I've become the go-to expert for national media on cheaters, sexters, marriage, divorce, sexuality, and a host of other human behaviors. At times, I've been called an evolutionary feminist because I believe women deserve freedom and equality—but not freedom from the demands of our perfect biology. Male and female biology are still not equal—and that's the omitted fact in many media messages about dating, mating, and relating. Be prepared: This book offers blunt, straight talk for progressive women.

Personally, I've lived nine lives of love. I'm a single mother who, at one time or another, has been a girlfriend, a wife, and a live-in love. Today, I'm raising two girls—one of whom just became a teenager. I'm not sure if she feels lucky to have a mom with my knowledge. But I guarantee she'll be very prepared for the dating scene when she enters it.

And so will you. *The 30-Day Love Detox* is part of a five-part attachment strategy. With old courting rituals gone, the detox is a way for you to create new ways to assess men. It's a step-by-step plan that will help you define a target mate, detox the bad boys, and choose the man who can't wait to close the deal with you.

Scientific research. Anthropological truths. And proven techniques. That's what sets *The 30-Day Love Detox* apart from any other relationship book. If nothing else, you'll leave the pages of this book with an understanding of the awesome power that lies within your female biology. You already own the race car, girl. I'm going to show you how to drive it so you can win the race.

PART I

THE
ATTRACTION
REACTION

The Dating Addiction

H is butt is what I remember. Smallish for a man but brown, tight, and brave. I remember it for one specific reason: That juicy nalgas was being hurriedly stuffed into a pair of pants and propelled out of our room at the W Hotel. My stomach churned out the meaning of all this. This man with whom I had had an intimate phone, text, and e-mail relationship for a year was running for the hills on a bright Sunday morning in New York after one of the best dates of my life! Whose hills? I still don't know.

What I do know is he came back. Not that day or that week. But he came back with words of apologies, dreams of a future together (mostly mine), and sturdy, vigorous sex. Oh, and he finally gifted me with clear words that he *can't* be monogamous. I wrote him off as boyfriend material long ago, but I watched his pattern. And I listen to similar stories from women.

"The guy I'm dating rarely calls, but when I go out of town, he texts me that he misses me," says one 28-year-old executive at a technology company. "Then, I come back and we go back to just having dinner and sex. I feel like maybe it's the technology thing. We don't ever just stay in and watch a movie. We don't ever talk about family."

In other words, men aren't willing to do the work of relationship building. And frequent technology check-ins make a pretend relationship feel real.

"The latest guy I'm with," says a bright 29-year-old who's a producer at a TV production company, "will text me every single day. It's like some kind of check-in. But for what? He never calls for a date."

"It's nauseating how much guys text!" adds another exasperated career woman. "And some of them are so lazy, they send group texts to a bunch of women when it gets late in the bar: 'Hey, babe. What are you doing later?' I guess the first woman to respond gets to hook up with his drunk ass."

"I've never been on a real date," admits a 25-year-old cosmetologist, who has been sexually active for 10 years. This attractive young woman has been having boyfriends and sex for a decade and no one has ever called, made the plan, picked her up, and paid for the evening. Her life is one of joining men at bars and parties. No man has ever courted her. It broke my heart to hear this.

These kinds of relationships are all too common today. Incoming men. Outgoing men. Men who dance around any conversation about commitment and always seem to get distracted by the high supply of sex available at such low cost. When we did a story on dating on *The Doctors* TV show, the single women we spoke with all told me that the biggest problem in dating today isn't *how* to meet a man but how to find one who'll *commit*. And by the way, women aren't even sure if they should be pressuring these men for more because, well, it's so much fun to date. Young career women are enjoying sex for sex's sake, and some are auditioning dozens of men for the coveted role of exclusive mate. It seems there's a ton of opportunities for love and sex these days. But at what cost?

LOVE A.D.D.

Have we become a culture with a severe case of Love Attention Deficit Disorder? Are we addicted to dating? In a word, yes. In our anxiety to attach or avoid attachment, we're running around using dating and sex as a drug. At a loss to identify what true feminine sexual freedom really means, many women have adopted a male model of sexuality. What's good for the gander is good for the goose. If he can sow his wild oats, she can too. While there are some good points to this newfound sexual freedom, there are also some serious drawbacks to America's new pastime.

I noticed that dating was becoming an epidemic a few years ago when I was living in Italy and had a foreign perspective of our game of musical beds. An Italian tour operator pointed this trend out to me over veal Milanese and fritto misto. His name was Maximo, and he looked like he had sprung from the pages of *Under the Tuscan Sun*. Tall, dark, with a heavenly accent, and chased by American female tourists—most of whom he thought were aggressive and crude.

In his mind, I was probably safer than most long-term tourists because I was with child. Well, actually, I was with two children. And they were not quietly tucked in my womb. I was a single mother. In Italy, that means I had unknowingly been transported from the category of "bella donna" to the untouchable status of "mamma mia." Lonely place, ladies. Clearly, Italians don't know what to do with a single mom. Apparently, no MILFs or desperate housewives among the olive groves. Anyway, thanks to my untouchable status, Maximo could freely speak to me. And because he travels to America a lot, he compared the two cultures.

"You want to know what Americans are obsessed with?" he asked me. I leaned forward. I did. I really did. Especially if this jewel of wisdom was served up with such a delectable accent.

"Two things," he continued. "Choking and dating." I blinked. I raised my slightly Botoxed eyebrows. And I jutted my chin forward as I waited for more.

"Everywhere you go in America, there are signs about choking hazards," he went on. "There are detailed diagrams in restaurants and public bathrooms explaining how to do the Heimlich maneuver. Do Americans not know how to chew their food?" He was as bewildered as I was. I had never thought of this. (Note to self: Teach kids to cut their food into small pieces.) But then came the other important Italian observation.

"And dating! Americans are obsessed with dating. There are dating TV shows. Dating Web sites. Dating experts. People in America date instead of fall in love."

There you have it. From the mouth of a hunk came the birth of this book. Clearly, we need more signs posted about dating hazards. Or we need to chew up our men more carefully.

America is obsessed with dating and mating. Dating has become an Internet commerce, a TV reality show darling, and a hobby for many, many people. But is it getting the intended results—the creation of intimate life partners? Is this dating craze—with its plethora of revolving dating partners, dating as TV entertainment, dating Web sites, and sex *without* dating—helping us find romantic partners who last more than a few months? I, for one, really don't think so.

We've gone from romancing and bonding to dancing and fondling. Not only are we addicted to dating, but we're addicted to a host of human behaviors that enable our dating addiction. We're addicted to texting, sexting, Facebook, shopping, gyms, and primping, and some people are even addicted to hookups. Clearly, Houston, we have a problem.

The High Price of Dating

None of this would be a problem if we all planned to live solo in our condom-stocked lofts and condos forever, making enough money so no one will ever have to clean a toilet or change a diaper. But most humans are wired to bond. And that desire to bond evolved so people could stay together long enough to water, fertilize, and grow the seed that often comes out of couples. Parenting is best played as a team sport.

"Our culture is not designed to teach women about motherhood," says Joan C. Williams, JD, a distinguished professor of law at the University of California at Hastings. In her book *Reshaping the Work-Family Debate: Why Men and Class Matter*, she maintains that most women underestimate the demands of motherhood.[1] "In the lower classes, parenthood and marriage have become two separate concepts, and having a baby is a rite of passage into adulthood," she told me. "And in the middle and upper classes, women are extremely focused on education and career, and when they hit the motherhood wall, their lives don't make sense anymore."

Thus, there's a problem with dating for sport rather than dating for partner research. Sooner or later, dating leads to babies for the vast majority of women. Eighty percent of women will become mothers—married or not and good boyfriend or not. And plenty of women simply don't understand the consequences of not choosing well.

Cases such as the one in Maine that involved missing baby Ayla garner national media attention not only because of the tragic nature of a missing infant but also because these explosive stories shine a light on our muddled relationships. Ayla went missing while in her father's care. Her distraught 20-something mother appeared with me on HLN's *Nancy Grace* show and was quick to explain that the baby's father wasn't her husband. He wasn't her ex-husband. Nor was he even her ex-boyfriend. "We were just friends," she said. "We were never together." Clearly, they were friends who had hooked up at least once.

On the most dire end of the scale, if dating can lead to a pregnancy where no one is clear on who's responsible, then on the other end of the scale, dating can lead to a painful broken heart—more often for the woman. Despite what feminist literature tells us about sex—that we can own our own orgasm and be happy and that that is enough—women have a pesky hormone called oxytocin that can bind our heart to a loser. I'll explain why in the next chapter, but for now, understand that women get painfully disappointed once they've attached their heart to something. In fact, it's that same disappointment that fuels the tear-thirsty audiences of dating reality shows. It can also lead to an STD—also more likely for women[2]—but you never hear about that on *The Bachelor*.

I mean, if the purpose of dating and mating had nothing to do with reproduction and the only thing you were interested in reproducing was your last earth-shattering orgasm, then there would be no problem. No problem for now, that is. Don't close this book if you clearly don't want children and you're under 30. I detested the little buggers myself until, oh, about age 32. And then I was slammed with a maternal urge that itched worse than a yeast infection.

Babies are often the little miracle problems that wiggle out of hookups, girlfriends, cohabiting unions, college sweethearts, and marriages. And then there's this 18-year unpaid labor called *parenthood* that mostly becomes the burden of women. In her book *The Richer Sex: How the New Majority of Female Breadwinners Is Transforming Sex, Love, and Family*, reporter Liza Mundy of the *Washington Post* described a "big flip" in gender roles. In her utopian world, men will become far more domesticated and women will be the breadwinners.[3] But not in this world. Not today in your current dating life. A review in the very paper Mundy writes for explains Mundy's optimistic data this way:

> Mundy may be right that more households will soon be supported by women rather than by men, but in part that is because more women are raising children without male support; few of these women qualify as "the richer sex." In addition, much of the growth in the share of income that wives contribute to households results from the long-term stagnation of men's wages. Thanks to the ban on pay and hiring discrimination over the past 40 years, women's average wages have risen from their much lower starting point, but they do not yet equal men's.

With 14 million single mothers currently raising one in four American babies,[4] it's clear we're usually left holding the bag—the *diaper* bag, that is. If you don't believe me, consider this statistic: One in four fathers lives apart from his children, and one-third of those haven't seen their kids in the past year.[5] In a year!

Women just aren't adapting to the hookup culture.[6] It defies our biology. As the hookup culture has burgeoned, female mental health problems have, too. In the past 15 years, depression rates in women have doubled and female suicide has tripled.[7] More proof is in the prescriptions. According to a government study, antidepressants have become the most commonly prescribed drugs in the United States. They're prescribed more than drugs to treat high blood pressure, high cholesterol, asthma, or headaches.[8] And they're overwhelmingly prescribed to women.

Healthy relationships aren't only beneficial to women. Men benefit too. Long-term couples live longer, have better health, and accumulate more wealth.[9]

Unfortunately, men didn't get this memo! Most men are happy to sail along making money and booty calls—leaving all the maternal problems and mental health issues to the strong, independent, efficient women. This is the tragedy of the sex-and-the-city mentality. We now have

Monogamy and Money

Based on 2009 Bureau of Labor Statistics figures, almost 40 percent of US working wives now outearn their husbands. A 2010 Cornell University study found that men are most likely to cheat when they're economically dependent on women.

four jobs—protector, provider, nester, and nurturer—and we seem to have no time anymore to be custodians of the social order.

High-Supply Sex and Low-Supply Families

When I pitched the concept for this book—how it would be different from any other relationship book ever!—I got more than a few jaded looks and eye rolls from veteran editors who had heard it all. But by the time I had finished talking, they were sitting up on their pretty coccyx and paying attention with jaws wide. And this is exactly what I told them:

Since 2010, in America, nearly half of American babies have been born out of wedlock—a more than 25 percent jump since 2002. This has occurred while the rate of teenage pregnancy has been going *down*.[10] So, who are these unwed mothers? They're live-in girlfriends, they're older single mothers, they're gay and bi gals, and some of them are just plain unexpectedly knocked up. And most of them are considered to be powerful women compared with women in other countries or women of other generations.

Why are we seeing this "breakdown" of the family? I'll explain later why all this change isn't necessarily bad for families, but for now, let's go with the less judgmental question of "Why are babies popping out in nests that look different from the traditional norm?"

The answer is that we're also seeing an unprecedented rise in the number of women in America who need marriage less. According to Brian Pendleton, sociology professor at the University of Akron, who has done decades of research on career women, "Women are finally beginning to realize they don't need men to define their worth."

Tell this to your bra-burning grandmother: Today, women hold unimagined power. First of all, our college campuses have become feminized. If you consider US-born 30- to 44-year-olds, women hold the majority of college degrees and are the majority of those with some college education but not a full degree. Women even make up three-fifths of graduate students. In the most common ages of marrying (ages 25 to 29), a record 36 percent of women hold bachelor degrees, while only 28 percent of their male peers can say the same.[11]

Women are also working and surging ahead with their careers. Because of the massive layoffs of expensive male employees during the great recession, we now have more women than men in the workforce.[12] We still need more stilettos in our boardrooms, but as far as employees go, we're now the majority in the American workforce. And in thirty-nine of the fifty biggest urban centers, 20-something, single, childless women are making more money than their male peers![13]

Yep, coming to a city near you: Men with no money to pay for dates. By the way, the greatest disparity is in the city of Atlanta, where young women make 21 percent more than their male counterparts. Not the city to date in if you're looking for a traditional marriage with a male pro-vider! But you may not be. This is the kind of thing we'll consider in Chapters 4 and 5.

Clearly, the rise of women is great news. Today's women have found freedom and independence that genera-tions of women before us only wished for. There they were, our grandmothers, trapped in a traditional gender cage, dreaming of paychecks, their own office, bills to pay, office politics to navigate, boring subway rides, long hours, and horrible bosses. Okay, so only some thought of the downside of a career. But what I promise you none of them considered was the reaction of men to the economic rise of women.

The Big Payback

Here's the payback: When women rise in power, men are less likely to get married and less likely to produce a big, uh, a big paycheck. Really. And it's all because sex is in such high supply in our culture.

Stay with me now. This is basic social anthropology. When women are disadvantaged or oppressed, they tend to use sex to survive. They either withhold it or sell it. And men compete for it. Disadvantaged women can't extract resources from the environment through gainful employment, but they can still extract resources from men. So, they close their legs until a man signs on the bottom line to support a woman and her offspring. It's called *marriage*. Even today, in countries where there are few opportunities for women, virginity is coveted. When women are given fewer educational and employment avenues, traditional marriage rates increase—often not by choice but by default.[14]

The other thing women do when they have little independence is to monetize their vaginas. Consider Victorian England. A time of great industrialization and growing prosperity—for men, that is. Sexual repression became the norm as women barely risked revealing an ankle before a man married them. But women in the lower classes survived by building businesses catering to upper-class men. It's estimated that during Victoria's reign in England, there was one prostitute for every 12 men.[15] Assuming not all men were patrons of ladies of the night, you can imagine that those hardworking girls had some steep competition for a narrow market. Ironically, as we've become addicted to dating and competing for a narrow market of men who'll commit, we also shop at a store called Victoria's Secret.

Here in America, traditional marriage rates are decreasing. About half of American adults are married now compared with nearly three-quarters in 1950. Women don't need traditional marriage economically and the sexual double standard is all but disappearing (I'll talk about the "all but" later), so women are finally free to enjoy the pleasures of their bodies. We can own our own orgasm, our own birth control, and our own boy toys. Yippee!

Here's the first payback: When sex is in high supply, men are less likely to commit.[16] I mean, why should a dude buy the cow when he can text in a herd for an orgy any night of the week? And when sex is in high supply, men also tend to become less ambitious and earn less money. In our hunter-gatherer past, the hunters who brought home large quantities of valuable protein got access to more women and higher-status women. In recent times, the men who lavished women with gifts and expensive dates got laid more often. But all that's needless today because women offer sex virtually for free.

The Backward Sexual Economy

Look no further than your average candlelit restaurant or Broadway show to see that women are courting men, not the reverse. At a recent Cirque du Soleil show, I saw a couple who looked to be in their early thirties. She was wearing a killer black cocktail dress and gold sparkling platform shoes. He was casually slunk in his seat wearing jeans and flip-flops. I mean, why should he even try? He knows he's likely getting laid. He has the upper hand in this backward sexual economy.

Indeed, there's a growing imbalance between the number of men and women. It's not that fewer boys are being born. It's that they're growing into fewer successful young men—compared with the number of successful young women. So women who want a committed relationship and a family with a man who stays around and helps are scrambling to compete for the narrow market of eligible male peers. And places where young people usually meet their mates, such as college, workplaces, etc., are now full of more women than men.

In her provocative book *Manning Up: How the Rise of Women Has Turned Men into Boys*, author Kay Hymowitz makes a startling case that there really are few good men out there, as most live as if life were a Judd Apatow movie (*Knocked Up, 40-Year-Old Virgin*).[17] She paints a picture of a pre-adult male who's delayed at growing up. When I posted a review of Hymowitz's book on my Facebook page, a mostly female comment stream dribbled down with sad testimony that the "pre-adult" male is very real: nearing 30, playing video games, laughing at frat house humor, with beer in hand and air escaping from his body. Sigh.

But despite all this role reversal, many American women still hold a mantasy that's better suited to the 1950s than this millennium. A 22-year-old business graduate student sounded like she was in a time warp when she relayed her plans to me: "I want to be engaged by 25, have three years of married life, then have four children and, when they are all in school full-time, go back to work."

Fifty years ago, by the age of 27, most men held a good job, had a mortgage, and were married.[18] Today, that description more closely matches the average woman, albeit without the wedding band. And that 27-year-old dude? In this decade, he's almost as likely to be living in his mother's basement with his Xbox and an iPhone, trying to get you to e-mail him a naked picture of yourself. I once met a 40-year-old man who spent his days this way. No joke. Mother's basement and all.

Another Complication: Our Girls Club

We've established that if you're looking for more than a romp and some companionship, there are fewer eligible men in the single marketplace. But there's another factor to consider too. There's far more female-to-female competition for those guys. Three types of women in particular are crowding the field.

First, there are your peer girlfriends who are also addicted to dating. This kind of competition isn't new, but their tactics are. They feel the competition, so they're pulling out all the stops. Or they aren't competing for mates and are just enjoying their sexual "freedom." Either way, your more adventurous girlfriends are spoiling your future boyfriend with frisky texts, e-mailed naked photos, and free sex. In the 2012 Harlequin Romance Report, 43 percent of single women admit to having sent a sext to a guy and 27 percent have texted a naked photo of herself. A friend of mine found a lost cell phone one day, and being a Good Samaritan, she scrolled through the device looking for the owner's contact information.

Instead, she found hundreds and hundreds of pictures of naked women! All this is causing a lot of confusion and distraction for men.[19]

Then, there are the MILFs—(Single) Mothers I'd Like to Finagle into my bed. Remember those 14 million single mothers who for one reason or another were left holding the diaper bag? Well, they're dating too. A mother's place used to be in the home, not the gym and the bar. But here they are—all around us: Mothers who are still on the market. And they would have been off the market if the donor whose sperm had latched onto an egg had also made a commitment to the egg's host. At no time in history have so many divorced and unwed mothers been vying for the same population of men as single never-married women.

And don't forget the cougars. Another by-product of the high divorce rate and our no-rules relationship revolution is the number of older single women who are looking for a hot, young guy. They can date your men because social mores against such behavior have lessened. And boy are they frisky! Women of a certain age actually have a heightened sex drive in response to their dwindling fertility. It's as if as the baby factory shuts down, it pummels an arsenal of hormones and the odd healthy egg down those Fallopian tubes—machine gun style. One study showed that "women with declining fertility think more about sex, have more frequent and intense sexual fantasies, are more willing to engage in sexual intercourse, and report actually engaging in sexual intercourse more frequently than women of other age groups."[20] Great. While you slave through graduate school and devote the time necessary to advance at work, some carefully manicured, sexually experienced Mrs. Robinson is tempting (or dating!) your current or future boyfriend.

Not only do cougars have chops in bed, but they're also

spoiling young men with their wallets. Many cougars are financially secure—either the product of a successful career or a successful divorce settlement. And that accumulated wealth is being sprinkled over young men—enough to keep them happy and lazy. The last thing many a young man who's hooking up with a cougar wants to think about is the financial pressure and sexual diet he would have to go on in order to marry a woman his own age.

One female college student I interviewed told me a heart-wrenching story about a guy she was so into. They had been "lightly dating" for a few weeks when he asked her to be his date at his own mother's wedding. She thought of this as a turning point in their relationship; she took this as a sign he was serious about her because he was ready to introduce her to his family. At this point in the story, her voice became tense and her eyes drilled into me. "At his mother's wedding," she declared, "my guy hooked up with his mom's friend!" Right in front of her eyes, her man had become a cougar's prey.

And if all this news isn't bad enough, you also have to compete with porn. Yes, with such easy access to pornography, women are being asked to do things in bed earlier than they might otherwise, and they're doing more risqué acts because guys now have a taste for excess. One New York playboy loves to ask young female dates if they ever "practiced bulimia" in college. Apparently, his sexual fetish is to use his appendage like the finger-down-the-throat method because he saw some porn that showed a woman barfing on a penis. To him, this is cool. Unbelievably, young women regularly accommodate him.

Clearly, the market for commitment-oriented men has been shrinking and the competition to lasso one has been increasing, but there's one more problem still for dating women: our time clock.

Ticking Wombs

Yes, we're educated. We have great incomes. We don't believe in a sexual double standard to shame us, and we have fabulous dates and boy toys. True, we have fewer marriageable men (read: men who'll commit and maybe even pay at least half the expenses) and much more competition among women, but overall, we feel empowered. But despite all this female power, there's one thing we can't improve on. We aren't *really* equal to men. We have a time problem. Men don't. (Although new research has shown that aging sperm is now linked to autism.)

Hymowitz explains the problem this way: "I think women have an implicit deadline to building up their careers. They know that decision [to have children] is coming. Men don't have that deadline. I've had men say to me, 'I'm a guy; I can wait 'til I'm 35 or 40.' And it's true. That means that pre-adult men and women are on different tracks. That's a source of stress between the sexes."

This may very well be the most pressing problem for women in the dating evolution. While it may be socially and morally okay to adopt a male model of sexuality, women are driving a very different race car—one that's going to run out of gas. Simply put, women have a fertility window and men don't. That means the music is going to stop for us in this game of musical beds, and it virtually *never* stops for men, who, thanks to Viagra, are still thinking with their small heads in old-age nursing homes.

A majority of young women's life plans still include motherhood. But most women are living with the fantasy that they can behave exactly like men in their twenties and then sometime in their thirties, when they're ready, they'll find a comfy, stable dude to settle down with who'll be a big provider. They think this while they're training men to do the exact opposite.

Here's the reality: Twenty percent of women older than 40 are childless. This number has grown by 80 percent since 1976.[21] Understandably, some women choose not to become mothers for any number of reasons. But many of these women *did* want to have children at some point. According to an analysis of data from the National Survey of Family Growth: "Among older women, ages 40 to 44, there are equal numbers of women who are childless by choice and those who would like children but cannot have them."[21]

For some, the problem is fertility. For others, the music never stopped in the game of musical dates. Or perhaps they wasted years with a "stringer"—the kind of man who dates or cohabitates for years with promises of a future together but never commits.

In her provocative book *What, No Baby? Why Women Are Losing the Freedom to Mother, and How They Can Get It Back*, author Leslie Cannold, PhD, interviewed hundreds of childless women, who reported the following reasons for not becoming mothers: "Requests for details brought out accounts of fertility difficulties, failed efforts to persuade childless partners, and frustration at relationship breakdowns that occurred just when children were being planned. It also brought matter-of-fact revelations of depression, anger, or sadness about childlessness."[23]

When I was 19, I saw a pop art greeting card with a caricature of a 1950s female face in great distress. The thought bubble above her head read: "I can't believe I forgot to have children!" Today, the same slogan is printed on cards, mugs, and T-shirts as a humorous nod to support the group of adults who have made a personal choice to not partake in parenthood. But when I saw that card, even at my young age—and I was on spring break in Key West, Florida!—it gave me pause. I remember standing in the card shop literally frozen in my tracks. This was a serious "note to self" moment.

Years later, on the New Year's Eve when I was single and 35, I had an epiphany and that "note to self" boomeranged into my consciousness and landed with a thud in my brain. I was standing at a fired-up New Year's Eve party at the Hard Rock Hotel in Las Vegas. I was with my old friend Ryan Seacrest, who was a different age, on a different track, and about to launch into superstardom. As the countdown to midnight ended and I surveyed the scene of hundreds of drunken young bodies exchanging wet kisses—and who knows what else!—I suddenly turned to Ryan and said, "I'm out." As I walked away from his confused face, I'm sure he thought I meant I was leaving this party to find another one. (Or maybe he was coming up with his famous "Seacrest out!" sign-off.)

But I wasn't going to another party. Instead, I was out of that life, the party stage of my youth, and the dating scene. I went home to my apartment in LA carrying that "note to self" in my brain. I didn't want to forget to have kids. Weeks later, I met the man who would become the father of my children. As a former athlete, he had good genes. I didn't have time to find out if he would be a good father or provider. We were pregnant within months. He stayed for a decade, too. These days, that ain't bad.

As parenthood goes, I feel like I got in just under the wire. I gave birth to my two daughters at age 36 and age 41. Lucky for me, I had no fertility problems or major pregnancy complications. I do wonder if the late age of her parents contributed to our daughter's autism spectrum diagnosis, but who knows?

The Fertility Scam

If many women in their twenties hold a fantasy that they can simply stop their addiction to dating when they're ready and choose to settle down with a marriageable guy, just as many also hold a fantasy about fertility. And this fantasy has been fueled by the marketing campaigns and success stories of fertility clinics. One California fertility clinic advertises an astounding 60 percent success rate, but when I called to inquire, they explained to me that that statistic applies to women under age 35 and refers to a success rate in becoming pregnant, not a live birth. Wow. I know enough women who have had devastating miscarriages to know that this isn't much of a promise.

For every success story you hear, there are thousands of women and couples for whom fertility treatments are unsuccessful. One woman I spoke with had spent close to $75,000 and seven long years trying treatments until she gave up. "I never expected this would happen to me. I thought I would grow up, get married, and have children like my mother. I had a career, but my dream was to be a mother. I felt like a failure."

Artificial insemination (yep, the turkey baster method) can cost up to $2,500 for each try. And the success rate is only 5 to 25 percent.[24] And if it does work, it could cost tens of thousands of dollars for multiple tries. That's if you're thinking sperm mobility is the problem.

Then, there's in vitro fertilization (the Petri dish baby, commonly known as IVF). The average cost in the United States is $13,775 per shot.[25] The success rate is 15 to 20 percent for women ages 38 to 40, and for women older than 40, it's as low as 6 percent.[26] That means at least 80 percent

Successful Women Are in High Supply

A study of 117 countries shows that when men outnumber women, marriage rates go up. But when women are in oversupply, an oversupply of sex occurs and more children are born out of wedlock.[27]

of the time, your $13,775 gets you nothing. Then, there are the medical complications that can rack up more costs. Laparoscopy used to extract eggs carries risks related to the anesthetic. Then, there are risks of infection, bleeding, and damage to the bowel, bladder, or a blood vessel. Surgery to repair damage can also be costly.

There's always adoption, but even though it can be easier on your body, it can also be costly and heartbreaking. I have a friend who has been attempting to adopt for years. Her life has become an emotional roller coaster: Every time she thinks an adoptive baby is on the horizon, some administrative complication dashes her hopes away.

Mary, a woman I spoke with in Colorado, felt she won the lottery when her name finally came up on the state list for an infant who matched her race (her preference). Colorado has a foster/adopt program, which means the hopeful adoptive parents actually raise the child until all the paperwork is finalized. I bet you know where I'm going here. The unthinkable happened. "We had him for two years and then something fell through the cracks. His biological family won parental rights. We had to give him back to sick parents. I couldn't stay in contact. It was too painful. I still can't imagine what happened to my little angel. I loved him so much."

The Love Detox

I warned you that this book would be a stone-cold look at the dating and mating market. I promised you a wincingly honest account of your situation. But none of my message should sound like I'm blaming women for anything.

If you're a woman who's single or divorced, it's simply not your fault. If you have no trouble meeting men but find few who'll commit, it's still not your fault. If you're one in five women in her forties who finds herself childless and gets caught up with shoulda, woulda, coulda, I'm here to yank you off that self-blame train.

Your predicament isn't caused by your choices. It's been caused by a shake-up of love's playing board that no one could have foreseen. I'm also here to assure you that love isn't dead. That monogamy is alive and well. Healthy, happy families still exist, and a huge population of great men and compassionate women are living in meaningful attachments. And great single men are waiting to meet you!

Gender roles have been changing. Financial arrangements have become nontraditional. But for the most part,

History of Dating

Dating in America began in the early 1800s as young people searched for mates. Back then, dating never involved sex. By the 1820s, the word *date* had become a euphemism for prostitution. One hundred years later, during the Jazz Age, dating became expected and encouraged for young people. Today, 80 percent of Americans have sex before their 19th birthday, but the average age of marriage is 27. Clearly, dating today involves sex.

know this: Most humans of both genders have an inherited urge to bond with peer lovers across their life spans. I'll talk about the evolution of love in the next chapter.

But this addiction to dating is another matter. Besides all the cultural factors I mentioned, I think so many women have entered the hookup culture out of anxiety. They think that in order to get a man to be their boyfriend, they have to join the high-supply sexual culture. There are other women who are simply reacting to the whims of their bodies or the whims of their egos or trying to heal an old psychological injury with a quick fix of a sexual drug. And despite what some feminists might tell you, an addiction to dating and sex that leads nowhere isn't freedom. It's an equality trap.

In the next chapter, I'm going to remind you about the amazing power of your feminine biology. I'll tell you why I think this culture of changing gender roles and changing sexuality is returning us to something more natural for our biology. (I'll even explain why what we consider a "traditional" family—à la the 1950s—is a somewhat insane environment for children to grow up in.) And after you gain a better understanding about what's natural for male and female biology, I'll give you the secrets that our hunter-gatherer female ancestors perfected when selecting mates in a high-supply sexual culture.

Commitment-oriented men who can be involved fathers are a depreciating demographic. But they're out there. And I'm going to tell you how and where to find them. I'm also going to tell you how to make a serious relationship life plan so you won't be left holding the bag if you don't want to. *The 30-Day Love Detox* will help you identify a commitment-oriented male partner who has the potential to be monogamous—and then show you how to apply the mating strategies to act like a wise, modern cavewoman.

CHAPTER 2

The Evolution of Eve

Okay, take a deep breath. I know the last chapter was a bit of a downer. But here's the good news: We may be experiencing an oversupply of successful women in our culture, but in our hunter-gatherer history, successful women have always been in high supply!

Women as second-class citizens is a recent phenomenon—a minor blip in our evolution, if you will.[1] The great female downfall may well have been the evolution of farming, where women became isolated from their super structure of supportive women and labor became divided by gender—as in, men went out in the fields and women stayed barefoot and pregnant in the kitchen.

But make no mistake about it. Since the beginning of

time, women have been more successful than men in extracting resources from the environment. In hunter-gatherer times, gatherers brought back about 80 percent of the calories to the village![2] And they were also skilled at choosing good men as protectors, providers, and fathers. Long before dating books, dating TV shows, and dating experts, women used the wisdom of their bodies and their quick minds to choose safe mates. Their lives literally depended on it. They also had to negotiate through a sea of reproductive imposters—men who look like fit mates but who are mostly trying to extract sex from women.

To understand why mate selection is so crucial to the survival of your genes, you must first truly understand women's historic roles and what our bodies have been wired to do. In this chapter, I'm going to explain the power of your unique feminine biology and the "natural" ways humans mated and parented for millions of years. Then, in the next few chapters, I'll explain how this cavewoman wisdom can be used today to select a good mate.

Hear Me Roar

I truly realized the power of women as I laid awake one night staring at a tiny, brand-new face that had popped out of my womb earlier in the day. I can honestly say—and most mothers would agree—that this was the most awesome event of my entire life. Even typing the words fourteen years later brings tears to my eyes. I continued to be astounded when I found that my body could also produce food for multiple humans for years on end. Who knew? And this is the very power that men unconsciously wish they had. Bottom line: Women give birth to life. We're next to godliness. And men spend a whole lot of time trying to trick us into believing they have the power.

The other female power men are all too conscious of is our sexual power. One bad-boy date let that cat out of the bag in a candlelit restaurant. Over sushi and sake, he confided to me that if women only knew the extreme gratification sex brings to men they would rule the world by holding their vaginas for ransom. He assured me that sex feels way better to men than women (I might argue with that) and that men will do nearly anything to obtain it. The release, the ego boost, the pleasure. He looked at me dead straight and declared: "Women have no idea."

Hold that thought, ladies, because that's going to be a big point in coming chapters, but for now, let's focus on other powers, such as resource extraction, social administration, and maternal power.

It was somewhere in the cloud of postpartum hormones and breastfeeding love that I realized I had been ignoring my powers for years. As a single woman, I had allowed men (and the women who collude with them) to define me based on looks or career success. No more startling was this realization than when I went for a walk with my three-month-old angel prize strapped to my chest. Who should I run into but a confirmed bachelor whom my gal pals had been chasing for years.

Seeing me with my baby, he strutted over to chat. After a cursory glance at my precious bundle, he moved up to my eyes. But rather than offering some words of congratulations about my healthy birth, he scrutinized my face and in an almost surprised tone said, "You look good."

As if motherhood somehow came with a prescription for ugly pills! He was still stuck on my value as a sex object and couldn't even acknowledge the fact that I was now a goddess. But the best part was my reaction. I laughed out loud and said: "Thanks, but who cares! I make people." And I sauntered off, singing a lullaby to my infant.

It didn't matter that he didn't get it. The best part about understanding the power of female biology is the fact that it fills you with self-confidence. That's partly because new mothers actually grow bigger brains, specifically in the areas linked to motivation. Research published by the American Psychological Association discovered that the brains of women who had recently given birth bulked up in areas linked to motivation and regulation of emotion.[3] Mothers become different people, literally.

Even if other people don't notice, you know it. And that same goddess power can be acquired when women without children use their nurturing power all over the planet, saving children, saving animals, and being nurturing custodians in the business world.

Self-Confidence Is Sexy

My main point is this: Why do you need to wait until you have a baby or give birth to a multinational corporation to understand the power of womanhood? What if you could have the power now? What if you could take a "new mother confidence" out on every date?

In the last chapter, I painted a somewhat dismal picture of the imbalance between the numbers of successful women and successful men. True, there's a shrinking population of men who'll commit, be monogamous, take an interest in their offspring, and make almost as much money as you do. But your first defense to this problem is self-confidence. Studies show that high self-esteem is attractive to both genders,[4] so why not put yourself at the top of the dating pool simply by loving yourself first?

If I knew you in person, I'd be happy to point out all the amazing, unique qualities that make you special. All the things you should feel proud of. Of course, I don't know you. (Although, if you see me, please introduce yourself!) But I do know a piece of you. I know your female ancestors—the ones who proudly walked the plains and forests tens of thousands of years ago, wearing babies, foraging for vital nutrition, and holding court as the backbone of our species. The blood of those women runs through your veins today. You're a product of specialized evolution. Whether you believe it was by intelligent design or natural selection, it doesn't matter. The power of woman lies within you.

The "Eve" of Evolution

First of all, know this: Your biology is ancient. Your Prius and your Jimmy Choos may be new, but they cart around a biological control panel that's designed for your survival. That's why you're here. You survived. All because your ancestors made some great choices. They didn't eat certain poison berries; they scooped up your ancestral baby grandmother off the forest floor before a lion came along; their strong bodies propelled them across continents to more fertile land; and, most importantly, the women in your past chose great mates. Healthy mate selection is the key to survival of the fittest. And you inherited the ability to choose well.

Look no further than the famous Swiss T-shirt study to understand how biology sometimes trumps culture.

Women were asked to smell some very fragrant T-shirts men had slept in every night for a week. The women were asked to determine which body odor was most attractive. When blood work was compared, it was determined that women were most attracted to the pheromones that signaled the most different immune system from themselves. Apparently, when sperm marries egg, certain features are taken from each partner: blue eyes from one, brown hair from another, etc. The exception is immune systems. When two people procreate, their immune systems combine and become stronger.[5] So, when you're sitting in that cocktail lounge wondering why a certain guy smells so yummy, you might consider his immune system. (But not if you're on the birth control pill, which seems to gum up nature's intelligent process.[6])

If you're still wondering how the DNA of that hunter-gatherer ancestor can help you find a meaningful relationship today, remember that she lives in you and has the capacity to operate for you. And she was a hunter-gatherer. For about three million years, humankind has lived by carrying out two basic activities: hunting and gathering. Hunting included fishing, and gathering included everything from roots and fruits to insects. We're very unusual compared with most other animals because we do both. We gals may look like attorneys, presidential candidates, or pilots, but in fact, we're hunter-gatherers.

The ways of a people have run in our blood for more than three million years. We became farmers only 7,500 years ago. And the industrial revolution was about 200 years ago. Two hundred years of new behaviors versus three million years of practice? Which do you think represents the hardwiring of our genes and behaviors? My bet is on ancient biological intelligence.

The Time When
Women Ruled

When I was talking out this book to my literary agent, my publisher, my girlfriends, and, basically, anyone who would listen, I was surprised to learn that many women still buy into a Hanna-Barbera version of our ancient ancestors. Well, actually something far more barbaric than the Flintstones. They picture a cavewoman being clubbed and dragged by the hair into some man's cave. Ladies, this couldn't be further from the truth. Newsflash: Throughout most of human history, there has always been a high supply of successful women. They differ from us in only one big way: They didn't give away sex so freely. Way back when, hunters were darned lucky if they were allowed into the female-run village. And to get in, they had better present some good protein as a hostess gift!

The Real
Traditional Family

It's a misnomer to refer to a traditional family as one heterosexual male married to one heterosexual female with offspring that have a genetic connection to both. This is an old-fashioned family. If you watch the TV show *Modern Family* or see the families that produced the kids of *Glee*, you know the old-fashioned family is giving way to a variety of postmodern families. Some of them look a lot like our ancestors.

First of all, know this: All human beings are born premature. The big trade-off for bipedalism—walking upright on two legs—was narrow hips. You may think your hips look big in your skinny jeans, but compared with your humanoid ancestors, you have very narrow supermodel hips. Now the only way to get a big-headed baby out of a set of narrow hips is to have a short pregnancy. It's as if Mother Nature said, "Get that thing out before it gets too big and Mama explodes!"

Thus, all human babies are born prematurely. Think about it. Most other animals are up and running with the pack within a few hours of birth. But not human babies. Human babies require a second pregnancy of sorts—an "in arms" phase of at least a year while the brain triples in size. Then, for another two to four years, toddlers must be carried, protected, and fed. In the past, all babies were breastfed for two to five years to sustain themselves with valuable protein until their molars came in and they could chomp on an animal leg. There were no blenders and certainly no packaged Gerber baby food for hunter-gatherer mothers.

So, who carried around that baby and kept the toddler from being eaten by predators? A multitude of related people. A real "traditional family"—the one that existed for millions of years—was more like a moving encampment of a few families. When the number rose above 35-ish members, some split off.

While there was no such thing as the "legal" marriage that we know today, there was certainly monogamy. Plenty of men hung around to protect their female partner during the vulnerable years of pregnancy and years of early child raising. There was also lots of love, bonding, and secure attachments going on. You'll hear more about that in a moment.

But first, let's talk about how the family looked. It was multigenerational. Older siblings, grandparents, and aunties and uncles were as likely to be helping to protect and nurture children as mothers. In her book *Mothers and Others: The Evolutionary Origins of Mutual Understanding*, renowned anthropologist Sarah Blaffer Hrdy, PhD, of the University of California at Davis calls these additional caregivers alloparents and says they were crucial to the evolution of our intelligence. According to Hrdy, this cooperative parenting stimulated our brains, emotions, and social structures by challenging an infant to decode a bunch of different faces and languages. She credits the alloparent system as one of the contributions to the amazing intelligence we have today. She also blows the lid off any notion that a "nuclear" family is anything but a recent invention by farming and industrialization. And she makes a clear case that early life exposure to *consistent* multiple attachments is the best thing for children. The wider the variety of consistent faces an infant has to decode and silently communicate with, the more likely that baby will grow up smarter.[7] (I put the word *consistent* in italics because attachment injuries, such as abandonment and separation from a loved one, even a beloved nanny, can be very damaging to children, and that kind of emotional stress prevents brains from developing to their fullest capacities.)

All Mothers Worked Outside the Home

The biggest misconception about hunters and gatherers is that men hunted and women gathered. In fact, that scenario was quite uncommon. Indeed, the hunter-gatherer societies that exist on the planet today provide great evidence of how the labor was divided.

While most of the gathering of wild fruits, vege-
tables, nuts, and insects was done by women, most gals
also hunted. And any hunter who would have walked
past a ripe patch of berries because he thought it was
"women's work" could become an empty-handed provider
at day's end.

Plenty of hunter-gatherer societies still exist today.
For example, in the Philippines, the Aeta boast many
women hunters. In fact, nearly 85 percent of Aeta women
hunt. When they hunt alone, they have a 31 percent rate of
successfully capturing game compared with men's 17 percent rate. But when those women join forces with a good
male hunter, their mutual success rate becomes 41 percent.[8]
That's why in Nambia, the women of the Ju/'hoansi people
work with male hunters as trackers.[9] I like to think of the
mythical Katniss Everdeen character from *The Hunger
Games* books and movies as a futuristic cavewoman. That
chick was great with a bow and arrow. And she did even
better when she went hunting with Gale. (Spoiler alert:
Skip the next sentence if you haven't finished *The Hunger
Games*!) But when we get to the chapter on men, you'll
understand why Katniss ended up picking another kind of
male to mate with.

Recent studies on group intelligence in workplaces
show that mixed gender groups are better at problem
solving than any single gender group.[10] So, when you're
thinking of successful mates, think *partner* over provider.
We're meant to complement each other. According to
anthropologist and archaeologist Steven Kuhn, PhD,
from the University of Arizona, a division of labor based
on sex is a recent invention.[11] It more likely evolved during the farming period when women moved from their
support system of extended family onto some hunter's
plot of land.

Not only did men and women behave more cooperatively, but they were also having more fun. According to prominent anthropologist Marshall Sahlins, hunter-gatherers worked far fewer hours and enjoyed more leisure time than most people today. And they still ate like kings.[12]

It's estimated that women gathered and hunted about twenty hours a week and all workplaces were baby friendly. They wore their babies to work. When babies became toddlers, there was an abundance of free child-care in the village.

The Grandmother Gene

Human females are unique for another reason. We're one of only three species on the planet to have menopause. Except for orca whales, pilot whales, and people, all other animals give birth until they die.

Let's think about this: Why would Mother Nature plan that we would live the last third of our lives as relatively healthy, wise, effective—and sterile? Anthropologists speculate that we evolved to have menopause so we would have grandmothers around to help with the next generation of offspring to increase their chances for survival. Remember, human babies take years to get on their feet. Thus, those mothers who had mothers who became sterile prematurely probably inherited that trait themselves. They and their kids were more likely to survive and have kids of their own who also inherited the "grandmother gene." Today, menopause is species wide. And that's why we have a narrow reproductive window. Nature has designed your body to get a healthy baby out on time so you'll have time to nurture the next generation of genes.

The Transitional Family

As we now know, the old-fashioned family that existed in the second half of the 20th century was a prescription for female depression. Imagine the 1950s and early 1960s (or just watch a couple episodes of *Mad Men*): One woman stranded in a tract house in the suburbs with a bunch of screaming kids while her hunter went to the office and on business trips. Yikes! And the helpful grandmother of the past might be far away in her Florida condo. No wonder Betty Friedan published the feminist manifesto *The Feminine Mystique* in 1963. Times certainly were bad for many women.[13]

I like to think of the twentieth century and the new millennium as a time of great family transition. By moving from the industrial age to the information age, women are regaining economic parity. As a result, families are changing. Forty percent of married households boast a wife who makes *more* than her husband. One-quarter of American children are being raised by a single mother, and loose networks of parents in various school communities are behaving very much like our multifamily clans of the past. Alloparents have stepped in—whether they're paid daycare workers, nannies, or people with a biological connection to a child.

As I write this, my kids and I are down with a flu bug. I'm a single mom, and if I were isolated, this would be a disaster. But I have carefully used my cavewoman wisdom to build a village over the last few years. A cousin came by to drive the only well child to school. A single dad from our school just brought us chicken soup and Gatorade. An alloparent woman who gets paid to help pitched in with cleaning. A working, single girlfriend sent over a pizza for dinner. This is my cavewoman village in action. And this is what we may be returning to in terms of family structure.

But there's still much choice. Families with a mom and dad who live together and wear wedding rings are still a slight majority, even if they may sometimes look a little different (maybe with a female breadwinner and a male nurturer). And they're still thriving, especially in faith-based communities and social circles where marriage contracts are connected to transition of wealth. The less money you make, the less likely you are to be married.[14]

While families are changing at a fast clip, research still supports the idea that today, a two-parent family with both partners having a biological interest in the child is the best prescription for successful kids.[15] One statistic that might be particularly startling to single mothers who fantasize about a blended family: One of the most dangerous places for a child in America today is living in a home with a nonbiologically related male. Yep, that's Mommy's boyfriend, husband, or stepson. Kids in this version of family have eight times the rate of emotional, physical, or sexual abuse.[16] That's not to say there aren't great stepfathers out there. It's just a cautionary note that single women with children need to be especially careful and vigilant when choosing a mate.

That's why I call this era a time of family transition. Families are evolving, but all the support systems of our hunter-gatherer communities aren't in place yet. Few women have an instant network of alloparents—grandparents, aunts, nieces, etc.—at their beck and call. Instead, we have expensive networks of childcare, including nannies, daycare, and preschools, that can set a mother back $15,000 to

$30,000 a year. Today, cavewomen must choose mates carefully and think logically about the consequences of choosing a certain kind of mate.

Women Are Dating Blindly

While there are plenty of different forms of family to consider down the road, many dating women haven't even figured out who they are or what they want as they consider various male partners. Instead, they're enjoying their sexual and financial freedom while holding a fantasy that an old-fashioned family will be available to them when they choose to settle down. Still others are afraid to acknowledge their feminine longing for a family. Said one 24-year-old teacher: "I always wanted to be a mother, but I never tell men that's what I want because I'm afraid they'd leave me."

But our high-supply sexual culture has changed the whole game. And many women—blind to the changes—are making outright dangerous decisions for their reproductive success. Anthropologists are scratching their heads over this. Why would women join a hookup culture that's dangerous for their mental and physical health and their reproductive success?

Women have so many family-style choices available to them. We can have a cohabiting relationship, a "stay over" relationship, a single mother family, a female breadwinner family, a peer marriage, or an old-fashioned marriage with a male breadwinner. But the key is to choose what's right for you rather than fall into something you didn't bargain for. Every one of these choices has pros and cons and trade-offs that many young women have yet to consider. Bombshell, ladies: Unless you understand the costs and benefits of each kind of relationship, you're playing Russian roulette with your genes. (I told you I'd be blunt!)

This book is ultimately about figuring out what *you* want, how much time you have to make it happen, and which kind of man will meet your needs. We'll get there. But first, let's talk about love and hookups.

The Evolution of Love

First of all, love is real. It's an event that has measurable emotional and physiological effects. It's an intoxicating emotion that evolved for one important reason: to create pair bonds that would endure long enough to protect and raise offspring. And there are plenty of stages and incarnations of love. I like to narrow them down to four specific kinds of love: sexual attraction love, romantic love, intellectual decision love, and mature companionship love.

Sexual attraction love is a biological response related to an attraction to the sight, sound, and smell of another person. It makes us want to touch and be with that person in a physically intimate way, and it affects our brain chemistry like an amazing drug. When we fall in love, our bodies release feel-good chemicals. These are often what make our palms sweat, our cheeks blush, and our hearts race. Many of the substances in our brains, such as dopamine, serotonin, epinephrine, and norepinephrine, increase with feelings of love, giving us a "love high." This is nearly identical to what happens when people are on drugs. Just like heroin, love lights up the pleasure center of the brain and feeds us feelings of euphoria. When we fall in love, blood flow increases in this area, which is the same part of the brain responsible for drug addiction and obsessive-compulsive disorders. This is one of the reasons that falling *out* of love (or getting the news that someone has fallen out of love with you) isn't always so easy.

Depending on how you see it, the good news—or the not-so-good news—is that our brains eventually begin to tolerate all these excess chemicals and then the "honeymoon" phase of our relationship ends. We're no longer lusting after our man, and the butterflies in our stomachs begin to subside. Then, hopefully, as we become more attached in our relationship, endorphins and the hormones vasopressin and oxytocin flood the body, giving us feelings of security.[17] If you made it this far, you've managed to move past the lusting phase and on to bigger and better romantic love.

Romantic love is sexual attraction taken to the next level. It involves fantasies about a future together and the delusion that this person is "perfect" for you. This is the brain's classic way of seeing someone as a soul mate. It may also involve cultural accessories, such as wine, chocolate, candlelight, and flowers—all things that pleasantly affect human senses and enhance the delusion. I use the word "delusion" on purpose. In the early stage of romantic love—which can last up to a year—couples high on dopamine and oxytocin tend to overemphasize their partners' good qualities and overlook their flaws.[18] Don't get me wrong: Romantic love is powerful stuff—it enhances our mood as well as our well-being. One study even showed that when people are in love, they're more creative.[19]

Then, the bubble bursts. By the end of the period of romantic love, people usually have made lifestyle changes based on the delusion that their partner is perfect. Circles of friends have merged, families have met, living arrangements may have changed, wedding invitations may be on order, and a pregnancy may even have happened. That's when our intellectual minds kick in with a cost-benefit analysis.

If the love is strong and the couple is thoughtful about their feelings, the third stage of love may evolve. I like to call this stage *intellectual decision love*. This is a love that has moved past the delusion. These lovers see the flaws in each other and accept them while also holding on to the positive perceptions that attracted them in the first place. The ability to manage this transformation is influenced by the timing of their initial sexual relationship and the sequence of commitment and sex. As they continue to grow closer in an emotional way, opening up the most tender and vulnerable parts of their psyches, they become truly intimate. Knowing the flaws in each other and assessing their lifestyle and goals, they make a rational decision to combine lives in order to create something they couldn't do alone.

Finally, if they're lucky, they'll reach *mature companionship love*. This stage of love involves less sexual attraction, less romance, and less intellectual work. Mature companionship love is part habit, part comfort, and all about shared lives. Studies show that married men live longer than single men, and this is partly because of the care they receive from a woman.[20] I told you we were really goddesses.

The Oldest Trade That Women Lose Every Time

Our cavewoman ancestors felt love. So did many of their male partners. This powerful emotion became the glue that kept both partners together long enough to get the kids up and out of the nest. Monogamy didn't often last until death do us part or even until the kids turned 18, but it was functional for a time. Sound familiar?

But here's the bad news about love. Most men can have sex without any emotional connection. Only some women can do this. In fact, the oldest trade in our species is the one where women attempt to trade sex for love. Women lose every time. In Dory Hollander's book *101 Lies Men Tell Women—And Why Women Believe Them*, she says the number one lie that men tell women is "I love you" in exchange for sex.[21] Bottom line: Most men compartmentalize sex and love. Of course, those compartments can merge, but rarely after just a few hookups. Renowned evolutionary psychology professor David Buss, PhD, at the University of Texas at Austin and Martie G. Haselton, PhD, at UCLA found that the greater number of previous sexual partners a man has, the more likely he is to quickly perceive diminished attractiveness in a woman after sexual intercourse for the first time. Sex simply doesn't lead to love for men. And if the guy is a player, it more often leads to outright disdain.

But one study of young women showed that more than half of young women think a hookup is a stepping-stone to a relationship.

More disturbing to me are women who have attempted to adopt a male model of sexuality and separate sex from love themselves. Granted, a minority of women aren't wired to bond through sex. They can behave like guys. Maybe they've biologically adapted or maybe that's just truly how they feel. Other gals manage to hook up by psychologically disassociating. They go into an altered state of consciousness where they can detach from their emotions, their body, or their environment. As in, "I won't let myself feel longing to attach. I won't be squeamish when he asks me to perform a sexual act I'm not comfortable with, and I don't even smell this nasty frat room!"

In more obvious pain are the gals who really feel the emotional ache of a hookup and pay the price of trying to be cool. A young female graduate student described it this way: "I can't even count the number of girlfriends who've come to me in tears that their one-night stand never called, never asked them out on a date, never sent flowers. Then, there are the girls who've dug themselves even deeper into the heartbreak hole—the girls that hook up with the same guy for several months, hoping and longing that one day, he'll commit. None of these girls end up with a commitment, a ring, or even a real date!"

The biological reason for all this is a pesky hormone called *oxytocin*. Oxytocin is the female bonding hormone. It's excreted in large doses during pregnancy, breastfeeding, and one other event: female orgasm.[22] Women are wired to bond through sex. This longing wasn't created by our imagination or patriarchy or a sexual double standard. It was created through millions of years of evolution to help our species survive. And through sexuality, women have been the custodians of the social order. Lately, it seems, women have quit their jobs as that kind of ruler.

The Hookup Myth

Here's another newsflash: The hookup culture—the one with throngs of singles engaging in a sexual free-for-all—doesn't really exist. There's a lot of talk about hookups and not a lot of action. One study of college campuses showed that students talked about no-strings-attached sex and assumed it was happening a whole lot more than it really was. For example, less than 37 percent of students from a University of Nebraska study had more than two hookups during the past year, but 90 percent of the students assumed that the "typical" student had at least that. And although almost everyone had heard the term *hookup,* almost half felt a hookup did not always involve sex.[23]

Men, of course, are the authors of this conspiracy. Our hunters have magical abilities when it comes to extracting sex from women. By spreading word of mouth about a hookup culture, they're attempting to influence their sexual targets by convincing them that their bodies' hesitation about sex isn't normal. Their tactic is to separate you from your girl pack and make you doubt the messages your cavewoman body is sending you.

But you can't blame the horny devils. They tend to overestimate women's comfort level with sex because they like sex soooo much. In one study, men reported higher comfort levels than women with all sexual behaviors. Those dudes also overestimated women's comfort levels, especially when it came to full-on intercourse and oral sex.[24] Men also tend to be far less discerning about whom they copulate with.

Why Sex Is Still a High-Risk Hobby for Women

No one had to tell our hunter-gatherer female ancestors that sex was a high-risk hobby. Back then, women died fairly frequently in childbirth. Others starved to death in harsh environments trying to feed a baby and themselves. Still others—the ones without protectors—were attacked by marauding males, who might also have harmed their children. Other mothers contracted diseases that made them infertile or killed them altogether. And plenty of others had a life of hardship when their male hunter chose not to stay around to provide and protect.

Like it or not, you inherited those cavewoman fears. They came by you as honestly as your fear of snakes. (While we're more likely today to die from an electrical shock versus a snake bite, most people will jump in terror at the sight of a snake before the sight of an electrical cable.) In the same way, we inherited cavewoman mating caution. When you feel that age-old ache in your stomach after you've had sex with a guy who still hasn't called back, that's your cavewoman talking to you. When you hesitate to have sex with a man who appears to be saying all the right things but something in your gut tells you to slow down, that's your cavewoman talking to you. When you hook up with a stranger at a party because you're drunk or before you're ready, that's you silencing your cavewoman. And you're playing a dangerous game with your genetic line.

Oh, I can hear the cries of my feminist sisters now: We're *not* cavewomen! We *are* modern women who own our own orgasms. We've made great advances in medicine, birth control, and economics. We just don't have the dangers cavewomen did.

Really?

I used to think that too—until I dug into the research. For starters, death rates during childbirth have been rising during the last decade. Out of every 100,000 pregnancies, 13 women die in childbirth.[25] And for all our advances in medicine, the United States still has one of the highest infant mortality rates in the world.

And how about this? A 2008 report from the Centers for Disease Control and Prevention said that by age 18, one in four girls already has a sexually transmitted disease. Some of those STDs are incurable. That same report showed that one in six Americans has genital herpes. And having herpes *doubles* your chance of getting HIV and

AIDS.[26] Women are already twice more likely than men to become infected with HIV through unprotected heterosexual intercourse, but having herpes makes this risk even higher.[27] Hookups are a Petri dish for germ sharing. A recent study by sociologist Anthony Paik at the University of Iowa showed that people involved in hookups are more likely to have more than one sexual partner at the same time.

And here's a fact to take your breath away. According to a National Vital Statistics Report, American women are gifted with two million unwanted pregnancies each year.[28] There are plenty more "unplanned" pregnancies, but two million babies are just plain unwanted. What a thought. It's hard enough to raise a surprise baby that comes at an inconvenient time but quite another burden to raise a child you don't want. Of course, today many unwanted babies are aborted, which exposes a woman to a whole other set of potential medical consequences.

"So?" you say. "Dr. Wendy, you just told us how powerful we are. Even if we end up pregnant and aren't prepared to have the baby, can't we get an abortion or have the baby, hire a nanny, and keep on going?"

Yes, you can—if you know the risks. This is where advertising has created false confidence in women. While our medical advancements help us make choices about our reproductive health, there's much misinformation floating around. For example, abortion may be legal in every state, but it's not always available, so some women still can't get access to it. And health insurance plans vary wildly about coverage, with most of them declining the procedure.

Lina wasn't so fortunate. Married and in her twenties, she found that a prior teenage abortion had caused scar tissue to build up in her tubes. After months of dealing with the side effects of fertility medications, she had a procedure and left the hospital with four embryos implanted inside her body.

"The worst part was knowing that the odds were that those four babies would likely die, but I was desperate," she told me. "I felt powerless and even guilty. When I started bleeding four weeks later, it was devastating. I thought I was the biggest failure. I couldn't conceive. And now I couldn't even do this right."

And as for single motherhood, plenty of single mothers will tell you that two women (Mom and a nanny) raising a child is easier than dealing with a baby *and* an uninvolved father—although nannies and daycare are expensive and something you need to financially plan for. We'll talk about this in Chapter 4.

But the data are still clear. Kids with absentee fathers are worse off than kids whose parents are unhappily married. Children with deadbeat dads have worse health, lower academic achievements, and as teenagers have more high-risk behavior. Bottom line: At this time in history, children living with two biological parents tend to be healthier than children who don't and are less likely to be suspended or expelled from school or to repeat a grade. They also have higher average grades. And this next statistic is particularly hard for me as a single mother raising girls: Children living with a single mother are more likely to become sexually active at a young age.[29]

Kids aside, single motherhood is a high-risk hobby for women, too. Single mothers have worse health than their married counterparts and are two to three times more likely to seek mental health services.

I'm a single mother (not by choice) who's all too aware of these statistics. In my case, I have made clear choices and sacrifices that put my children first so I can offset these negative statistics. I spend a lot of time doing homework with my kids, driving them to educational activities, cooking nutritious meals, and keeping a very regular schedule. I feel it's my responsibility to do the work of two parents. I can do this because my happiness isn't something separate from my kids. My children's happiness *is* my happiness.

But do most American women see it this way? According to the media, a woman is expected to get back into her skinny jeans, her office, and her BMW six weeks after giving birth. And this anti-cavewoman behavior is reinforced with words of congratulations from other women who mistakenly think this is an accomplishment. It makes it hard to fault a woman for not being deeply emotionally entwined with her children when the early bonding period is cut short.

I once got in a spirited argument on TV with conservative author and commentator Ann Coulter on this very topic. She claimed that single mothers are bad for society and even implied that my daughters have a darned good chance of growing up to be strippers! Of course, I argued that even one good solid parent is better than two bad parents. But we were arguing about the wrong thing. Single mothers aren't bad for society. The lack of cultural support for families is bad for society—inadequate daycare and short parental leaves. That's bad for society. We've deprived ourselves of the very valuable cavewoman village of alloparents.

My point to you dating women is that your choice of male mate will directly impact your health, your wealth, and the success of your children. Selecting a boyfriend is so much more than hooking up with a deep-voiced stud with six-pack abs. Dating a slick, rich playboy may feel cool until he goes broke paying off baby mamas because he's a born cheater. And that sweet artistic type? The one who woos you in his loft? Unless he's got a business head, you may be underwriting his artistic "hobby" while raising his children. Are you really ready for that? If so, plan accordingly.

Your risks may be a little different from those of your cavewoman ancestors, but they're risks nonetheless. And in the next chapter, I'm going to ask you to take a hard look at yourself first. I'm going to ask you to purge inappropriate men. And I'm going to ask you to choose the kind of man your cavewoman ancestors would be proud of. He doesn't have to be a traditional male, and your relationship doesn't have to be old-fashioned. But he's gotta be right for you and your family plans. Or he's gotta go.

Survival of the Smartest Women

In the next five chapters, we begin your detox. It's a five-part attachment strategy that will help you beat the odds of finding a secure attachment when successful men are in low supply and high-risk sex is in high supply. We'll start by taking a look at you. Who you are separate from these bizarre cultural statistics. I'll ask you to take a few quizzes to find out about your education, your beliefs about gender, your finances, your attachment style, your religious beliefs, your politics, and your family system. By the end of that chapter, you're going to have a clear picture of yourself as a romantic partner. Then comes the pencil and scratch pad work. I'm going to ask you to make a relationship life plan—one that includes a timeline and a budget. Make no mistake. Your cavewoman ancestors counted the fruit in their bags before they set off on the savanna to find a cute hunter.

After that, we're going to talk seriously about men. All kinds of men. We'll identify the type exactly suited for your unique romantic style and your life plan. Then, we'll begin the purge. All inappropriate men will be cast away as you increase your chances for attachment and reproductive success. Finally, I'll explain a little bit about relationship systems. I mean, once you have him, you need to know what to do with him, right? Keep reading. Your 30-day love detox starts right now.

PART II

THE
FIVE-STEP
ATTACHMENT
STRATEGY

CHAPTER 3

Your Love Style

Sharyn is a 33-year-old mergers and acquisitions executive for an international brokerage firm based in New York City. She considers herself liberal and progressive and doesn't think she has any sexual hang-ups or a hankering for a relationship based on old-fashioned gender stereotypes. But she has noticed one thing about herself: She just does better in life when she's in a relationship. Her career goes better. She's more entrepreneurial, more creative, and even exercises more.

Love, I tell her, can definitely be life enhancing. Noted author and poet Diane Ackerman often writes about the intersection of science and love. In a *New York Times* article, "The Brain on Love," she describes the magical powers of a trusting relationship this way: "During idylls of safety, when your brain knows you're with someone you can trust, it needn't waste precious resources coping with stressors or menace. Instead it may spend its lifeblood learning new things or fine-tuning the process of healing."[1]

But Sharyn's current environment doesn't necessarily provide a steady stream of suitors offering the kind of trusting relationships Ackerman writes about. Her eyes become intense as she sweeps her long brown hair off her shoulders. A thick strand gets caught in one gold hoop earring as she leans in to explain this to me: "I know this sounds weird, but I thought I'd be at least living with a boyfriend by now. And I do meet a lot of guys. But mostly they want to keep up a Facebook, text, and Twitter communication and then just meet once in a while for dates and sex. What's wrong with me?"

I assure her that probably nothing is wrong with her except the fact she's a single woman living in a high-supply sexual economy. Sadly, the default strategy for women who are feeling an often unrecognized competition crunch is to play a game of musical beds in hopes they'll hit a relationship jackpot. (Or they're using the high-supply economy to live out a kind of attachment disorder you'll hear about in a minute.)

But this plan often backfires. The more sexual partners a woman has had, the more likely she is to be on an antidepressant.[2] It's important to add here that this statistic may work in reverse. In other words, the more depressed a woman is, the more likely she is to be using sex as a self-medication. But it's certainly not a far reach to suggest that the high-supply sexual environment is messing with women's predispositions to bond and contributing to all three behaviors: sexual promiscuity, depression, and antidepressant use. In my opinion, it's one big vicious cycle.

True, it may feel like bad luck to find yourself dating and mating at this time in history, but it's not a foregone conclusion that all women will lose. In fact, most women are still winning the mating game—but only the ones brave enough to do it on their own terms. In this climate, women who want a lengthy bonded relationship or motherhood with a dude at her side can't be content to simply "own their own orgasm." Women have to be prepared to "own their own love life."

Making Your Own Luck

Finding a solid mate involves some degree of karma, but you have far more control than you might imagine. Think of it this way: When hapless tourists gamble in Las Vegas, they most often lose. But professional gamblers who frequent Vegas are known to have big wins because they choose the casino and game table carefully. They also don't risk big money on a game until they learn everything there is to know about that game's odds. In some ways, *The 30-Day Love Detox* is an oddsmaker. It'll help you determine the type of man you're most likely to "win," and it will teach you how to play the game by using the right time frame and location to find him.

But you can't do it if you don't know yourself first. Even if the best gambler knows the odds, she has to understand her own vulnerabilities: Are you impulsive and reactionary when you lose a game? Do you play like a man but feel like a woman? Are you susceptible to the distraction of an attractive dealer? And, most importantly, do you know when to fold your cards and leave the table? These are the kinds of traits we'll examine in this chapter—your love style.

Your love style is no different from your gambling style. Do you love like a pro or a tourist? Are you impulsive and reactionary after a breakup? Do you behave cool and nonclingy when you'd prefer a clearer definition of your dating relationship? Do you secretly wish for traditional gender roles, or are you fine being the breadwinner? Are you susceptible to bad boys? Do you stick with a dead-end relationship and hope it will change? Do you use short-term sexual strategies and hope for long-term rewards?

A Case for Rational Love

If all this feels too clinical, too scientific, and way too unromantic, consider this: Romantic love has actually been one of the factors that helped keep women submissive and oppressed. Historically, if women focused on love and romance and held the perception that their mate felt the same way, it made it a whole lot easier to fold a pile of laundry or to prepare his martini when he came in the door after work. It made it easier to turn and look away when he was abusive or cheating. Women believed that romantic love was paramount to their survival.

Brian Pendleton, PhD, is a sociologist at the University of Akron in Ohio. From his vantage point at a Midwest college, he has been charting the progression of women and their relationships for more than thirty years. He's particularly fascinated with the high levels of education that droves of women are attaining; he says this is changing the way we love.

"Ever since the Industrial Revolution (around 1900), we have moved from rational love to romantic love. With women becoming more educated, we are swinging back to rational love," says Pendleton.

Our cavewomen ancestors depended on rational love to keep them and their offspring alive. Remember, their smart decisions are why you're here today. And this is what we're returning to.

The difference between romantic love and rational love is an awareness of power and choice among the heady rush of dopamine and sex hormones. If romantic love is based on chance and the total immersion in sexual attraction, rational love is based on self-control and sound decision-making skills. Both can be hot and exciting, but rational love is unleashed in a calculated, responsible fashion. In fact, research shows that relationships that begin with hot sexual chemistry often have the worst long-term outcomes. Relationships that begin with a friendship score higher in happiness, faithfulness, and longevity.[3]

Smart women have been engaging in rational love for centuries. Women who "marry up" think of love as a choice instead of a lottery win. These women may appear to be social climbers, but they choose to unleash their passion and sexuality on men who exhibit signs of being a good provider—whether through money or social connections (or both). However, the number of financially successful men is dwindling. Liza Mundy, author of *The Richer Sex*, interviewed women in the mating marketplace today who are choosing to "marry down" by selecting their mates based on domestic skills and fatherhood potential rather than income.[4] Mundy's subjects still deeply love, trust, and respect their husbands, but make no mistake, they've engaged in rational love.

Finding Your Love Style

Your love psychology is made up of a cocktail of beliefs that swim around your conscious and unconscious and sometimes cause your stomach to feel anxiety or euphoria. Many of these beliefs may be out of your awareness. For example, you have beliefs about attachment—how emotionally close or distant you like your mate. You also have beliefs about sexuality; you have a comfort level with a certain pace and menu of activities, even if you haven't been dictating them in your current dating life. And you have beliefs about gender roles; separate from what the media tells you about a "gender neutral" utopia, you have a gender role road map that feels good to you.

Understanding these three aspects of your love style will help you make a relationship life plan. We'll talk more about how to make that plan and stick to it in upcoming chapters, but first, let's find out who you really are as a mate.

In the next few pages, you'll find questions that help you begin to understand your own love style. Three well-respected tests used by psychologists and mating researchers will help you understand your attachment style, your sexual strategies, and your gender role comfort level. This is an insider's look at your love style. It will help you make clear, rational, timely choices to better increase your chances of finding the kind of mate you desire.

I encourage you to take your time with this. Think about it. Talk it out with your friends, family, and/or therapist. Be as honest as you can. This is your chance to identify the mate inside yourself. After you complete these questions and tests, we'll move on to making your personal relationship life plan. *The 30-Day Love Detox* is in many ways a relationship "diet" book. The first part of your attachment strategy is to count your current caloric intake (your love style) and then design a diet that's perfect for you (your relationship life plan) and then add that crucial exercise component (the detox), learn maintenance strategies, and make the detox part of your lifestyle—so you don't waste calories on junk food again!

The Science of Attachment

Perhaps the most fascinating area of mating research is an area of psychology and neuroscience called *attachment theory*. And it's closely linked to our cavewomen wiring.

The theory suggests that akin to animal imprinting, all humans have inherited an impulse to bond for survival. If hunter-gatherer babies hadn't clung to their parents, they would have been gobbled up by a predator. Like little ducklings who wiggle-waggle in a line following their mothers to the pond, humans wiggle-waggle through our adult relationships based on the imprinting of our early life caregivers. A childhood marked by loving, attentive, consistent parenting tends to produce an adult who trusts love and seeks out reliable partners. On the other hand, a childhood clouded with abuse, neglect, and inconsistent parenting tends to produce an adult with either a lot of anxiety about relationships or a tendency to avoid intimacy like the plague.

It's important to make a distinction here between sexual intimacy and emotional intimacy—the kind of open, vulnerable honesty that creates empathy and a lover's bond. Sexual intimacy isn't always connected to emotional intimacy. Being open with your body isn't the same as being open with your heart. But as you'll learn after you complete the sexual relationships questionnaire, there's a strong link between sexual strategies and your comfort level with emotional intimacy.

Early life attachments create a kind of blueprint for love. But the problem is this: Whether their attachment style is insecure or not, all those cute, little, imprinted ducklings grow up to become well-dressed men and women who mix and mingle in bars and message each other on Facebook. And no one can tell who's who! Men and women with insecure attachment styles—who avoid tender talk and commitment—are still wired to obtain sex. And they've figured out the minimum amount of words needed to accomplish that. (Note to Mark Zuckerberg: A relationship status tells us little about someone's ability to bond.)

Anthony Paik, PhD, of the University of Iowa, studies dating and hookups and finds them fascinating. His research shows that plenty of people date even if they aren't interested in long-term relationships—that is, even if they don't have a romantic attachment style that makes them want to have a relationship.

Paik says: "In the casual dating category, some people think they're headed for a long-term relationship, but there are also people who are only in it for sex. It basically brings 'players' and 'nonplayers' together. As a consequence, it raises the question of whether casual dating is a useful institution."

My answer to Dr. Paik is simple. Casual dating *isn't* useful. But formal dating with the eye of a schooled investigator can be helpful. Sadly, attachment insecurity seems to be fueling our addiction to dating and hooking up. The population of people who can easily form secure attachments (and give and receive care comfortably) seems to be giving way to a population of people with fears of abandonment or those squeamish about emotional honesty.

"I hate guys who call all the time," says one college student I spoke with. She rattled off textbook rationalizations for her apparent emotional avoidance. "Clingy guys are awful. Just text me the facts and we'll meet when we can. I don't need to hear about your day."

Other women I interviewed had similar, although heartbreaking, strategies to manage a different kind of emotional anxiety: fears of abandonment. Said a 26-year-old teacher: "I have completely shut off my longing for a relationship because if men don't know you actually want a relationship, then they might stay."

So, how common are people with attachment insecurity? Omri Gillath, PhD, is an associate professor in the department of psychology and the Hoglund Brain Imaging Center at the University of Kansas. His lifework sits at the intersection of love and biology, where he uses neuroimaging and gene mapping to explain connections between attachment style and mating.

When I asked him about the numbers of people in the American population with an insecure attachment style, he told me that people who can't easily form secure attachments make up about 40 to 45 percent of the population. Yep. That means almost half the guys you date have a challenging attachment style. They can talk about hopes for marriage or a long-term commitment, but they just can't get there. These men are either vigilantly staving off threats of abandonment by being controlling or jealous or they're regularly ducking out of a conversation—or your life—when things get a little too close. According to Dr. Gillath, "Perhaps most important for women is the fact that having an anxiously attached partner seems to have all sorts of negative outcomes, because avoidant men behave in line with their gender role." What he's saying is that the more traditionally masculine the man, the more likely he is to have attachment problems. And masculine men tend to be very sexually attractive.

Worse news: Some of the women reading this book right now also get anxious when it comes to men—vigilantly watching for signs of abandonment or avoiding closeness. Let's face it, love is emotionally risky. Opening your heart also means exposing yourself to the possibility of rejection—the most painful kind. It makes us vulnerable. Many of the women I interviewed for this book told me they were afraid to ask the man they're sleeping with if he could be referred to as their "boyfriend" because it might scare him off. This clearly shows the amount of power men currently have in our sexual marketplace, but it also alludes to how painful and debilitating abandonment anxiety can be.

According to Dr. Gillath, attachment anxiety and emotional avoidance are fueling our addiction to dating. "We know from our studies that insecure people—and especially avoidant individuals—tend to prefer short-term, less committed sexual relationships. I also have some preliminary evidence to show that people in the U.S. are gradually becoming more avoidant (due to things such as high mobility as well as low personal and economic security). Put these things together and you get the increase in hooking up."

The first goal of the five-part attachment strategy is to understand your own love style. Romantic attachment style is one important piece. Men and women who have a secure attachment style tend to seek out long, stable, satisfying relationships that are selfless and void of game playing. When determining someone's attachment style, researchers find it helpful to look at the proportion of anxiety and avoidance that person experiences in relation to emotional intimacy. Allow yourself about twenty minutes in total and grab a calculator because scoring might remind you of your third-grade math class. Enjoy your internal exploration.

The Experiences in Close Relationships-Revised (ECR-R) Questionnaire[5]

The statements below concern how you feel in emotionally intimate relationships. Answer the questions in terms of how you *generally* experience relationships, not just in what's happening in a current relationship.

Respond to each statement by giving a number from 1 (strongly disagree) through 7 (strongly agree) to indicate how much you agree or disagree with the statement.

____ **1.** It's not difficult for me to get close to my partner.

____ **2.** I often worry my partner won't want to stay with me.

____ **3.** I often worry my partner doesn't really love me.

____ **4.** It helps to turn to my romantic partner in times of need.

____ **5.** I often wish my partner's feelings for me were as strong as my feelings for him or her.

____ **6.** I worry a lot about my relationships.

____ **7.** I feel comfortable depending on romantic partners.

____ **8.** When I show my feelings for romantic partners, I'm afraid they won't feel the same about me.

____ **9.** I rarely worry about my partner leaving me.

____ **10.** My partner only seems to notice me when I'm angry.

____ **11.** I talk things over with my partner

____ **12.** I don't often worry about being abandoned.

____ **13.** My romantic partner makes me doubt myself.

_____ **14.** I find that my partner(s) don't want to get as close as I'd like.

_____ **15.** I'm afraid I'll lose my partner's love.

_____ **16.** My desire to be very close sometimes scares people away.

_____ **17.** I worry I won't measure up to other people.

_____ **18.** I find it easy to depend on romantic partners.

_____ **19.** I prefer not to show a partner how I feel deep down.

_____ **20.** I feel comfortable sharing my private thoughts and feelings with my partner.

_____ **21.** I worry romantic partners won't care about me as much as I care about them.

_____ **22.** I find it difficult to allow myself to depend on romantic partners.

_____ **23.** I'm afraid that once a romantic partner gets to know me, he or she won't like who I really am.

_____ **24.** I'm very comfortable being close to romantic partners.

_____ **25.** I don't feel comfortable opening up to romantic partners.

_____ **26.** I prefer not to be too close to romantic partners.

_____ **27.** I get uncomfortable when a romantic partner wants to be very close.

_____ **28.** I find it relatively easy to get close to my partner.

_____ **29.** I usually discuss my problems and concerns with my partner.

_____ **30.** I tell my partner just about everything.

_____ **31.** Sometimes, romantic partners change their feelings about me for no apparent reason.

_____ **32.** When my partner is out of sight, I worry he or she might become interested in someone else.

_____ **33.** I'm nervous when partners get too close to me.

_____ **34.** It's easy for me to be affectionate with my partner.

_____ **35.** It makes me mad when I don't get the affection and support I need from my partner.

_____ **36.** My partner really understands me and my needs.

HOW TO SCORE THE QUIZ:

1. To begin scoring, some answers need to be reverse-scored like this: 1 = 7; 2 = 6; 3 = 5; 4 = 4; 5 = 3; 6 = 2; and 7 = 1. Take all the numerical answers to the following questions and give them a reversed score: 1, 4, 7, 9, 11, 12, 18, 20, 24, 28, 29, 30, 34, 36.

2. Next, take the scores to all the following question numbers and average them. These are the questions you should average: 2, 3, 5, 6, 8, 9, 10, 12, 13, 14, 15, 16, 17, 21, 23, 31, 32, 35. In case you're rusty on third-grade math, that means add them all together and divide by the number of answers—in this case, 18. This is your score for attachment-related anxiety. It can range from 1 through 7. The higher the number, the more anxious you are about relationships.

3. Finally, take the scores to the following questions and average them: 1, 4, 7, 11, 18, 19, 20, 22, 24, 25, 26, 27, 28, 29, 30, 33, 34, 36. So, add up all the scores and divide by 18 again. This score indicates your attachment-related avoidance. The higher the score, the more you avoid intimacy in relationships.

Understanding Your Attachment Style

I think we all have a bit of anxiousness and avoidance when it comes to new relationships. We worry he's not going to call. We stress about whether he could be dating other women. We want him to know us, but sometimes, we hold back our true feelings. And when he opens up too much too soon, a red flag goes up that he could be a clinger.

New relationships are fragile, and some of this is normal. But if you scored particularly high on anxiousness or avoidance, when you think about how you generally experience relationships, there's much information here for you.

WOMEN WHO AVOID FEELINGS

Women who score high on avoidance have a particularly hard time feeling emotionally intimate. They don't like to talk about feelings and think a man is weak if he can talk about his. If this is you, you might find yourself behaving in ways that push a guy away when he gets too close. I knew one woman who would start fights over nothing whenever her relationship was smooth and tender. I knew another woman who would start dating other guys when her boyfriend got too serious. And I knew another who would give her boyfriend the silent treatment for days to avoid talking out a problem. These women all drove their men crazy with their inconsistent, emotionally avoidant behavior.

The challenge for women who are avoidant—yet still desire a long-term relationship and motherhood—is to become aware of patterns that sabotage intimacy. Once you're aware, it becomes a matter of choosing men who can help you open up. (Choosing a man who's also avoidant is like the blind leading the blind.) Once you have a dude you

Decoding Emotional Language

Having trouble labeling that uneasy feeling in your stomach? Here's my handy dictionary of the most common feelings people express. I like to call them the twenty power words of emotional intimacy. Next time you tell a story to someone, add your emotional experience by saying "I felt" followed by one of these words:

Nervous	Lonely
Happy	Excited
Sad	Surprised
Angry	Proud
Disappointed	Scared
Hopeful	Guilty
Ignored	Aroused
Embarrassed	Uncomfortable
Envious	Rejected
Jealous	Loved

This kind of language will open the door to the most tender parts of your psyche and help you become more accessible and, ultimately, more loved. It will also help your dates model their skills after yours. Using emotional language is a bit terrifying at first, but trust me, it can enrich all your relationships.

can trust, you'll need to start with small personal disclosures and build up your intimacy tolerance. The first step in learning to express your feelings is to simply explain to your date how hard it is for you to talk about your feelings. If you've picked well, this will cue him to be open and receptive to your baby steps of disclosures. And it's always good to practice first on girlfriends and other people with whom you have trusting relationships.

WOMEN WHO WORRY ABOUT LOVE

On the other hand, if you scored much higher on the anxiousness scale, you've got to do the work of containing yourself. Your preoccupation with a guy can sabotage things even before they begin. If you find yourself Facebook-stalking too much (we all do it sometimes!), sneaking peeks at his texts and call logs, or counting the days and hours between each of his messages and calls, you probably lean toward the anxious side.

Perhaps the most dangerous part of having an anxious attachment style is that we often invite the very thing we fear: a guy who abandons us in a critical moment of need. Women who are anxious about relationships tend to be attracted to these bad boys. I know this because I used to be one. If a guy was inconsistent, chronically late, or a potential cheater, I was ready to date him. I'm finally cured after seven years of psychotherapy and caring, bonded relationships with my children. But you can start now by asking yourself this: Do you find yourself male-bashing a lot because the men you date let you down? Then, this might be the time to ask why you were attracted to him in the first place.

Three Healing Relationships

The good news about attachment injuries is that your attachment style can change during your life span—for worse or better. I mentioned that the hookup culture and our addiction to dating are making people more avoidant, but let's talk about the better side.

Psychologists have identified three relationships that have the power to heal the damaged child within us. The most obvious, of course, is a therapeutic relationship. In the safety of a private and confidential office, a therapist can become a container for our most shameful memories and thoughts and a presence whose consistency can help rewire our brain.[6] The infant inside can imagine that "Mommy" will always be wise, stalwart, and compassionate—every Tuesday at 3:00 p.m. Consistency is one mechanism for healing.

Another valuable relationship is the one we can have with our own children.[7] If we're able to break the family cycle of family dysfunction and parent our children the way we wish we had been, parent *and* child can benefit. Every time a parent encourages, soothes, and assures a young child, words echo in the adult's head like a long-lost parent. Through our ability to give love, we're soothing and consoling ourselves at the same time. It's really amazing.

Finally, psychologists give credit to the romantic relationship as a powerful healer.[8] If we're fortunate enough to choose a partner who has an ability to fill in some of the gaps of our childhood, we can be fortified. Too often, though, people have a compulsion to repeat, and we choose the very pattern that injured us in the first place. At other times, even a relatively happy adult relationship can feel absolutely terrifying, especially if happiness and caring are foreign to the child within us. I encourage you to take some emotional risks in your relationships—to look closely at your tendency to recoil from care or withhold affection—because authentic love can feel scary. Authentic love isn't a perpetual happy place, but it's a home for the heart—one that creaks with age and burns with an internal fire. Love is the thing that makes us whole.

Your Sexual Style

Here's a mythbuster: Despite what the media portrays, women today don't have much sexual freedom. Don't get me wrong. Women are having plenty of sex, but they aren't really *free*. They're being pressured by a high-supply sexual economy to adopt a male model of sexuality while not acting too much like a man. Two sociological forces are putting women in a damned-if-you-do, damned-if-you-don't double bind.

The first problem is the sexual double standard. Most men still believe there are two kinds of women: "sluts" and women who would make good girlfriends.[9] Many of the young women I interviewed were less concerned with their sexual freedom and more concerned with their "count"—or the number of sexual partners they've had.

"I was e-mailing a guy I hadn't even met yet, and he asked me how many men I'd been with," said a 23-year-old engineering student. "I felt like I had to lie because my number is kind of high. I kept hoping I would meet the one guy who would be different—who wouldn't judge me on my number."

The second problem is this: Virginity and abstinence are ridiculed by both men and women. In this high-supply sexual culture, women who choose to control their output in the marketplace are subtly or overtly pressured to put out.

"A guy told me I was frigid. He told me I had a sexual problem because I wouldn't sleep with him," sighed a 24-year-old film production assistant. "He made me feel bad about myself. It was so confusing."

Far from having sexual freedom, women are being forced into a narrow band of sexual behavior. The message in our culture is definitely mixed: Have plenty of not-too-much sex.

As a result, women use an inconsistent mix of sexual strategies, and many have lost sight of their goal: to date as a selector for long-term love. I can honestly say the biggest dating mistake women make is to use short-term strategies for long-term goals. Dressing overly sexy and having sex too soon thwarts the chances for real love.

Test Number Two

The sexual relationships questionnaire beginning on page 74 will help you determine if you prefer short-term or long-term sexual strategies. The important point here is to know yourself and know what you want. You may find you prefer both or neither. This information will become important to you in the next chapter when you create your relationship life plan.

Understanding Your Sexual Style

Researchers often use the quiz on page 74 in conjunction with other psychological tests because it's closely associated with attachment style. And you might be surprised to learn that romantic attachment style and sexual strategies are closely linked.

If you score high on short-term sexual strategies, you're less likely to fall in love and more likely to get involved in relationship game-playing—the kinds of games that bring you closer to a man's manhood but not his heart. People who score high on short-term strategies also tend to be emotionally avoidant. And avoidant people actually fear

(continued on page 76)

Sexual Relationships Questionnaire[10]

The following items refer to sexual relationships. Please use the scale provided to indicate how much you agree or disagree with each item, keeping in mind the type of relationship in which you would prefer to have sex.

1: **Disagree strongly**

2: **Disagree**

3: **Neutral/mixed**

4: **Agree**

5: **Agree strongly**

———**1.** I'd like to have an ongoing relationship, assuming it was with the right partner.

——— **2.** I have no objection to "casual" sex as long as I like the person I'm having sex with.

——— **3.** I'm not really interested in forming a serious relationship right now, even if a seemingly "right" person comes along.

——— **4.** Sex without love is okay.

——— **5.** I'd love to be closely attached to someone (emotionally and psychologically) before I could feel comfortable and fully enjoy having sex with that person.

——— **6.** I'd very much like to find a serious relationship I could be sure would last.

——— **7.** It's okay to have sex outside the confines of a primary relationship.

———— **8.** I can imagine myself being comfortable and enjoying "casual" sex with different partners.

———— **9.** I'm not really interested right now in a long-term relationship with just one partner.

———— **10.** Any relationship I get into I would like to be serious and long lasting.

HOW TO SCORE THE QUIZ:

1. Reverse the scores for questions 3, 5, and 9. Again, this means $1 = 5$; $2 = 4$; $3 = 3$; $4 = 2$; and $5 = 1$.

2. Now find the average score for 1, 3, 6, 9, and 10. Hint: Add up all these scores and divide by 5. Here's your long-term mating strategies score.

3. Then, find the average score for 2, 4, 5, 7, and 8. Again, add up all these scores and divide by 5. This is your short-term mating strategies score.

closeness. You might show a greater preference for noninti- mate sex, such as anal sex and oral sex, and reach for that remote or dash to the bathroom to avoid after-play cud- dling. You also might be more likely to drink or use drugs before having sex to numb the stress over emotional inti- macy. You sometimes have sex just for the bragging rights and talk openly in your social circle about your conquests.[11] For you, sex isn't about expressing warm, loving feelings for your partner. But if he's rich, famous, or exceptionally hot, sex can be a way for you to gain social status.

If you score high on the long-term strategies, you likely have a secure attachment style. You're able to be selfless, and you're likely to move away from dates who play head games. You're open sexually and less worried about which one of you initiates. You enjoy physical contact, affection, and wild sex but mostly in the context of an exclusive relationship.

If you score high on both strategies, this might be a sign you're more anxious and preoccupied with your rela- tionships. You desire intense intimacy and want to be loved deeply. You often become obsessed with your big crush. The reason you have sex is less related to personal pleasure and more often related to a need to feel attached and attended to and to allay fears of abandonment.[12] You often have sex before a relationship is solid because you fear he will leave you if you make him wait.

Long-Term Mates Parading as Short-Term Girlfriends

All this talk about individual attachments can be clouded, morphed, and manipulated by one thing: the high-supply sexual economy. Research shows that these days, even securely attached women are using short-term strategies to obtain sex. They're participating in unwanted sex and performing sexual acts they feel uncomfortable with.[13] They're doing this because they're pressured to conform to peer messages from a mysterious—and mostly nonexistent—hookup culture. Some women think using short-term sexual strategies (dressing sexy, having sex too soon, or having sex without feelings) is normal. And this is quietly turning psychologically healthy, emotionally secure women into anxious, promiscuous women.

If you prefer short-term strategies, watch out for that slippery slope. People with the greatest number of past sexual partners are the most likely to form hookups and report lower relationship quality.[14] In other words, the more you hook up, the longer you're looking for something that doesn't exist.

"Those associations are there. Individuals with more partners do not tend to find these relationships that rewarding. Why is that?" muses Dr. Paik. "One answer is that they are built that way. This could be related to their belief about what sex is about. In the old system, they didn't have that much opportunity. The other explanation is that these experiences change their beliefs. We don't know. Is this a cause and effect? Is that brain pattern they are observing a cause or effect?"

I believe we're observing a cause. Short-term sexual relationships make one prone to more short-term relationships and less satisfaction. We know the Internet is training our brains to become super adept at scanning pages and impulsively looking for a click-through rather than taking the time to read an entire book. In the same way, multiple sexual partners train us for rapid, less intimate relationships instead of allowing us to take the time to read a partner fully.

The Gender Role Piece

I mentioned in Chapter 2 that we're in an era of family transition. A slight majority of children are still born into couples with a traditional legal marriage. But within those marriages and all the cohabiting unions out there are a variety of gender roles that women and men are laying claim to. In my interviews with women and my years in private practice, I was surprised to notice that most women don't give a whole lot of thought to gender roles—until it's too late. And that's mainly because thanks to feminist progress in education and careers, single women share the same gender roles as single men. They are equal and, in my opinion, the same gender.

But the problems start when that other gender enters the house—a mother. When two people come together to share housekeeping, childcare, and breadwinning duties, the rubber hits the pavement, and women are faced with shocking biological facts: Men can't have babies. And men can't breastfeed. And plenty of them, frankly, can't be good mothers. I've counseled more than a few weeping first-time mothers in my practice who find themselves deeply envious of their partner's freedom and feel trapped and over-whelmed by motherhood. It's something the most modern, very well-educated woman just isn't prepared for. Harvard Business School doesn't offer a class in nighttime parenting and breastfeeding.

In Chapter 5, we'll take a look at the wide variety of men out there: the providers, the fixers, the nurturers, the thinkers. You'll recognize which one is right for you after you take the next quiz. The dual-career family scale was developed back in the 1980s when women began to really enter the workforce in droves, and it asked women how they feel about gender roles. It's perhaps more apropos today because young, single women have simply stopped asking themselves these questions. For many, it's a foregone conclusion that the man they fall in love with will match their needs at home. But do you know what your needs really are? There's so little talk in our culture about feminine women who actually like homemaking and child-rearing. In fact, those women are often discriminated against—certainly in workplaces but also in educational and social circles where female progress is always judged by a male comparison. Take the test on the next few pages to find out if you'd be a better mate to a traditional man or a modern homemaking man.

Feminine Freedom

Some of you may feel these questions are downright old-fashioned. Our modern media spins delightful statistics about women and careers but rarely probes the challenges of motherhood and marriage.

And the misinformation begins early. At the beginning of her life, a young American girl is fed dreams of Disney brides and Prince Charmings, and by college, her life script seems to have been rewritten by a Harvard MBA. How confusing!

"We are at a moment of social flux," says Joan C. Williams, JD, a distinguished professor of law at the University of California at Hastings and author of *Reshaping the Work-Family Debate: Why Men and Class Matter*. "Marriage has become a luxury good. It's alive and well in the upper classes. But in the middle classes, it's on the run.

(continued on page 84)

Understanding Your Gender Style (Adapted from the Dual-Career Family Scale[15])

Please insert the number that indicates the extent to which you agree or disagree with the item.

1: **Strongly agree**

2: **Agree**

3: **No opinion**

4: **Disagree**

5: **Strongly disagree**

Marriage Type

_____**1.** If my child were ill and needed to remain home from school, I'd be more likely to stay home with him or her than my mate would.

_____**2.** Given the structure of our society, it's important that the woman assume primary responsibility for the care of small children.

_____**3.** I want my future mate to be the main breadwinner in the family.

_____**4.** My income will be as vital to the well-being of our family as is my mate's.

_____**5.** I wouldn't work if my mate didn't approve.

_____**6.** I wouldn't attend a professional convention if it inconvenienced my mate's work.

Domestic Responsibility

_____ **7.** Although I'll welcome my mate's help, I think the responsibility for homemaking tasks will be primarily mine.

_____ **8.** If a mother feels she's not meeting her domestic responsibilities due to her career involvement, she should cut back her career demands.

_____ **9.** I'll try not to make demands on my mate that his colleagues wouldn't have to meet.

Satisfaction

_____ **10.** I'd be a less fulfilled person without my experience of family life.

_____ **11.** Having children isn't a priority for me.

_____ **12.** My career is fulfilling, but I feel it doesn't satisfy me totally without children.

Self-Image

_____ **13.** Having a career will make me a better mate than I'd be otherwise.

_____ **14.** Married professional women have the best of two worlds: professional employment combined with a full family life.

_____ **15.** I think my career will make me a better mother than I otherwise would be.

_____ **16.** I hope to spend as much or more actual time with my children as my nonworking neighbors who are active in community affairs.

Career Salience

_____ **17.** I view my work more as a job than as a career.

_____ **18.** If my work were cutting into my family life and my husband could support us, I'd cut back.

_____ **19.** My career should be as important to my husband as it is to me.

_____ **20.** I'm as career-oriented as my male colleagues.

_____ **21.** I'd recommend that any young woman contemplating a career complete her professional training before marriage.

_____ **22.** In the case of conflicting demands, a professional woman's primary responsibility is to her husband and children.

_____ **23.** It's possible for a husband and wife to work in separate cities to maximize career possibilities and have a successful marriage at the same time.

_____ **24.** If I were to receive an exceptional job offer in another city (one I wanted to accept), I wouldn't expect my husband to accompany me unless he was sure of a suitable position for himself.

Career Line

_____ **25.** A married woman's career history should be considered in light of the two sets of demands she faces as a wife and as a professional.

_____ **26.** Most single career women have greater opportunities to succeed in a profession than do married career women.

_____ **27.** A married woman's career goals tend to be more modest than those of her male colleagues.

_____ **28.** I'd cut back on my career involvement in order to meet the needs of my family.

_____ **29.** I think my career would suffer due to the responsibilities I'll have as a mother.

_____ **30.** It's impossible in our present society to combine a career in the fullest sense of the term (uninterrupted, full-time work with a high degree of commitment and desire for success) with the demands of a family.

_____ **31.** I consider myself a working woman (have professional employment) rather than a career woman (to whom advancement and exceptional achievement in a profession are important).

HOW TO SCORE THE QUIZ:

1. Reverse the scores for questions 4, 11, 13, 15, 20, 21, 23, 24, 25, and 26. This means if you wrote down a number 1, change it to a 5. A score of 2 becomes a 4 and so on.

2. Now add up the scores of all 31 questions and then divide by 31 to find your average score.

3. A response below 3 is considered "domestic/traditional" and anything above 3 would be "career oriented."

Middle-class white families are starting to look like families of the poor, where parenthood and marriage have become two separate things. And upper-class women are so focused on education and career that motherhood becomes a crisis."

That's why I asked you to ponder those "old-fashioned" questions on the dual-career family scale—because they address all the mini-crises you'll face when you have a sick child, a job transfer, expensive childcare costs, and a home to maintain. And they directly impact the kind of man you should target.

If you found your score was on the high side—a 4 or a 5, meaning you value career over domestic life and motherhood—know that it doesn't mean you're not nurturing. Many women who choose not to have children become mothers of our culture, founding charities, shaping politics, and running compassionate corporations. I know I'd be a lost and struggling single mother without my village of girlfriends who aren't biological parents.

On the other hand, if your score was on the low side, indicating you have domestic, maternal needs, then embrace your inner goddess. You might have to look a little harder for a traditional man and extend your hunting ground to so-called red states and to religious communities, but if you stay true to yourself and your plans, you'll find a man who complements you as a wife and mother. I promise.

Having It All

Of course, the most common aspiration of American women is the notion that women can have it all—a career, a husband, a family, a great home. I like to say that women certainly can have it all—but not all at the same time. The superwoman myth of the 1990s has given way to a culture of balance and careful planning. Which brings me to the next chapter. Bring the scores from the three tests you just took. You'll need them as we shape a working plan for how to choose the right relationship for your life.

CHAPTER 4

Your Relationship Life Plan

"I'm so looking forward to that," said a single, 26-year-old real estate agent when I told her my attempts to set up our interview had been way-laid due to the obligations of motherhood.

I'm not sure she completely understood what I really meant when I said, "Sorry, I was busy with the kids." Did she know that my three-day delay involved one 4:30 a.m. start, six stints as a chauffeur, seven meal preparations, three loads of laundry, two parent-teacher conferences, a cheer-leading competition, and a 3-D science project—all while I maintained a career in media? (I admit, my nails lost out.)

I'm not complaining. I love my life and my kids. But does this young woman really know what she's "so looking forward to"? In short, has she made a *plan* for it?

Survival of the Planners

Women are excellent planners. For example, we make great educational plans. My 13-year-old daughter told me the other day exactly what her undergraduate and graduate school majors were going to be. And she listed every summer extra-curricular program that would make her application to a prestigious university look really good. These days, girls have moved from planning a prom to planning a serious education.

Women also make great financial plans. We can tell you exactly how many pairs of Christian Louboutin shoes we must deny ourselves in order to save for a down payment on a home. We can tell you the exact date our student loan will be paid off. And we can also explain why our socially conscious investment portfolio outperformed the market last year. We love spreadsheets.

We also make great wedding plans. Traditional marriage may be on the decline, but you'd never know it if you looked at the bridal industry. The average wedding budget has grown year after year and today stands at $27,021.[1] Women don't miss a beat when they talk about cut, color, clarity, Vera Wang, Monique Lhuillier, Swarovski, or the ring pillow and flower girl basket. And women make these elaborate plans all while working on a Yale economics thesis or studying for their medical board exams.

But so many women aren't good *relationship* planners. They leave to chance the most important decision of their lives by not asking the really necessary questions. For example, do you plan on having a traditional marriage or a cohabiting peer relationship? Do you plan on having children? If so, how many? Have you made a financial plan to be a single mother? Have your checked your clock and calculated your fertility window to determine when your plan needs to go into action?

And what about the kind of man who'll have a supporting role in this relationship plan? Will he share the chores or be a big provider? Is he a "type" according a list of criteria or are you still holding a somewhat archaic notion that a soul mate will magically appear as destiny? Might you be searching endlessly through bars, bookstores, and bedrooms for the one you think you're "intended" to be with, or might it make sense to be a bit more pragmatic about which kind of man will fit into your plan?

Love Doesn't Just Happen

I can't tell you how many women in my interviews said, "I want to be married. I hope it happens for me."

Newsflash for you smart, fabulous, ambitious women: Nothing else in your wonderful life "just happened." You made it happen. You made an educational plan and/or a financial plan and now you need to start making a realistic relationship plan.

What's a relationship plan? It's a plan that involves a timeline, a partner profile, a commitment strategy, a motherhood goal, a gender role goal, and a financial schedule. It's Life 101. I know. They didn't teach us this in school.

Here's a secret: Smart women have already been doing it for thousands of years. Our cavewomen ancestors chose good hunters in times of famine, good inventors (Remember fire? The wheel?) during fruitful times, great protectors during warring times, and great artists and musicians when *she* excelled at hunting. If Grandma was youngish and sisters were aplenty, women had more children. When a good brother offered protection to her offspring, our gatherer may have risked venturing further afield. When the environment became harsh, producing few calories or posing treacherous weather, women quietly crossed their legs until conditions improved.

So, if our cavewomen ancestors fell in love with rational choices, why can't we? Why can't we place as much importance on our relationship goals as we do on our financial goals? Remember, our choice of mate can determine the course of our lives. Consider the stories of the women below who mostly let love "just happen." Some won. Some lost.

Five Women—Five Choices

....

Candace married her college sweetheart: a law student. But while she took time off as an engineer to stay home and breastfeed her second infant, Candace found a family credit card statement with hotel charges that confirmed she'd been dealt a bad hand: Her husband was cheating. They divorced. Fortunately, she got to stay in the house, and because of his high income as a corporate lawyer, she receives enough child support to afford a nanny while she continues with her own career. But she's angry he's out having fun dating while she's left holding the diaper bag.

Willow was a working actress with frequent roles in TV and film. The guy she fell for was a supertalented graphic artist. Since they made about the same salary and there were no religious or parental pressures, they cohabited. Within a few years, they had two children. Willow had always planned to continue with her career but was unprepared for the overwhelming desire to nurture that took over her body after the birth of her babies. After baby number two, she stopped working altogether to be a supermom and assumed that Daddy would step it up in the financial department. That's when the fighting began. He had only signed up for the 50/50 relationship plan and refused to pay a penny more. Today, she's a single mother with zero child support. To say she's struggling is an understatement.

Sandra finally got her on-again, off-again, emotionally avoidant bad boy to marry her. It was a quickie wedding in Atlantic City when she finally had him in the right mood. She was thrilled. They built a giant house in New Jersey, even putting a stork in the tile of the future children's bathroom. But Mr. Bad Boy was also Mr. Control Freak, and he kept putting off the idea of getting pregnant. One day, her fertility window quietly closed. He refused to adopt. They eventually divorced. The tiled stork remains in the bathroom to remind her about her loss.

Marcia married a total peer. Both physicians, they met in med school in San Francisco. Marcia had been raised by a single mother and was determined to avoid those hardships. Before she married her husband, she laid out a very clear plan of the career-family gender roles. And the couple has stuck to their agreement. They share care of their four children and their house, and they function as true partners. What's more, she has a solid voice in all the household decisions because she established her voice early on in the relationship. They aren't rich by any means because their careers have been scaled back to allow for such a busy—but mutually rewarding—family life.

Finally, Liana had a great career as a local news reporter. But an early marriage and baby left her divorced and a single mother by age 22. Knowing the odds were against her to find a mate, she went into overdrive. Her friends laughingly dubbed her "the wedding planner." She had invitations printed and monogrammed napkins ordered for three separate grooms—each of whom got last-minute cold feet. Her friends said she was pressuring men and scaring them off. Undaunted, she poured her broken heart out to a male seatmate on an airplane. By the end of the flight, they were a budding couple, and by the end of the year, he showed up at the altar. Today, they live in a rambling home in south Florida with her teenager and their two additional little kids. Who's laughing now?

These are all real women. Their names may have been changed, but their stories are true and important. Of the five women, Marcia and Liana were clearly the planners. Both had learned from the negative experiences in the past—Marcia's struggling single mother and Liana's early hardship—which may have given them clear goals and boundaries. But it was also their firm ideas of who they were and what they wanted that helped them steer steadily along their relationship paths and accomplish their goals.

What's a Relationship Plan?

Creating a relationship plan is simple mathematics. It involves calculating the number of children you want, the financial contributions of a mate (or not), the number of years you have left to conceive, and the price of childcare and/or fertility medicine. Once your plan is made, we'll look back at how you scored on the three tests of attachment, sexual strategies, and gender roles to see if your love style matches your plan. For example, if you're 33 years old with a secure attachment style and a goal to have three children but you're using the short-term sexual strategies you learned in college, you might want to change your behavior and your target man.

In the next chapter, we'll talk about the wide range of male mates available to you, but first, let's create your relationship life plan.

My Relationship Life Plan

Marriage/Family Goal (Check one.)

___ I don't want to live with someone if we're not married.

___ I'll live with someone but won't have children unless we're legally married.

___ I'm comfortable being part of a cohabiting couple who are parents.

___ I plan to be a single mother without a partner.

Children (Check one.)

___ I hope to have more than two kids.

___ I hope to have one or two kids.

___ I already have kids at home and want more.

___ I have kids at home and don't want or can't have any more.

___ My factory is closed and I have an empty nest.

___ I don't want any children.

Fertility Window Calculator

(Skip ahead to "Politics" if you don't want kids.)

Age of first menstruation: _____

Add 30 years (average woman's reproductive life span): _____

Subtract your current age: _____

Years available to have a biological baby: _____

On your life budget, add $13,000 per child for possible fertility procedures if you plan to begin past age 35.

Education

___ I have completed all the education I need for my career.

___ I still have ___ number of years of education left.

Realistic Fertility Window: _____ (Subtract the number of years of remaining education from the years available to have a biological baby.)

Reproduction (Check one.)

___ I want only biological children and won't use fertility medicine.

___ I can easily see myself adopting a baby.

___ I want only biological children and I can afford fertility medicine.

Politics

___ I consider myself to be conservative.

___ I consider myself to be a moderate conservative.

___ I'm a conservative liberal.

___ I'm liberal.

Religion

___ My faith is very important to me.

___ I think of myself as more spiritual than religious.

_____ I believe I should follow all the rules of my church.

_____ I'd have difficulty being in a relationship with someone outside my religion.

_____ I hold my beliefs dear but can respect and have a relationship with a man who has different beliefs.

SCORES FROM CHAPTER 3:

Your romantic attachment style: _____

Your sexual strategy style: _____

Your gender style: _____

Making Your Plan

I want you to look closely at how you completed the relationship plan. If you know you want to have children (and how many), then you know exactly how many years you have to accomplish that. If you plan to have a traditional marriage and time isn't of the essence, you may want to add one to two years of relationship building before any child might show up.

Look at your romantic attachment style and your sexual strategy style. If you're anxious or avoidant and use a short-term sexual strategy, you've got two choices. If you're content with your past relationship patterns and don't plan on attempting a bonded relationship with children (insecure attachment styles can be passed down to children), then by all means continue with your life. Enjoy short-term relationships with partners who are doing the same. Take all the necessary precautions to prevent sexually transmitted diseases and pregnancy and live life to your fullest potential.

Carol did this. She had a successful career in public relations, a bevy of boy toys, and a life of laughter. She didn't want children, and with so many expendable resources, she had a killer wardrobe and a lifetime of luxury vacations. When she received the devastating news of terminal breast cancer at 54, she even planned her own funeral—the music, the speeches, the food and wine. And when she passed away, that carefully planned funeral went off without a hitch. To celebrate her, a troop of her current and past young boyfriends sang her praises at her funeral. What a life!

In order to enjoy her life the way she did, Carol acknowledged she wasn't truly interested in long-term love, marriage, and children. This self-awareness is key. If, like Carol, you're not wired to want a committed, intimate, long-term relationship, your relationship plan may look very different from other women's, and that's perfectly okay.

But if underneath your unhappiness you really do seek a committed, intimate, long-term relationship, you have another choice, which is to become healed and secure enough to create a healthy relationship. That kind of healing work starts with this book, and it may continue with a therapist depending on your needs. Professional therapy can be expensive and a long-term commitment of its own, but in my experience, it's made me a better thinker, more aware of my feelings, and certainly a much better mother.

If marriage and children are on your relationship life plan and your attachment and sexual strategies are steering you toward something else, this is the time to get a grip—to step off the painful roller coaster of short-term passionate rides and learn to take love slowly and carefully. You deserve the love you need.

Politics, Religion, and Race

If you're still working through some of the questions on my quiz and trying to decipher the meaning of it all, you might be wondering, why did Dr. Walsh ask about politics and religion?

First, while it's exciting to run with a pack of exotic men with wildly divergent values—"opposites attract"—it may not always lead to committed love. According to new research from Rice University and the University of Nebraska at Lincoln, people tend to be most attracted to those with similar political beliefs.[2] In fact, being liberal or conservative rated higher in importance than looks or personality in the choice of a mate. And yet politics is one of the least-asked-about questions on dates.[3] The more similar people are in their family backgrounds, life goals, and political and religious values, the more likely they are to stay together.[4]

With that said, I support interfaith and interracial couples. My own children are multiracial, and our family breakup had little to do with race. Marrying outside of one's race used to be associated with a social class change. Fifty years ago, skin color had a closer connection to economic potential. But thanks to education, immigration, and social progress, there are now wide variances of races within each social class. A Latino physician can meet her Asian spouse in med school. A white man can meet a black woman in law school. An Indian woman can meet a Middle Eastern boyfriend in her MBA program. And they'll all have similar values because they come from similar social classes. I especially encourage black women, who statistically prefer black men, to look outside their race for a mate. Seventy percent of black women are unmarried.

Vice President Mom and Gender

Look at how you scored on the dual-career family scale. Whether you scored more "domestic/traditional" or "career oriented" should tell you a lot about yourself. Now look at your age, the length of your fertility window, and the number of children you hope to have. Does this make sense? If you scored more "career oriented" yet you want a traditional marriage and more than two children, this will directly affect the type of man you should be dating. If you're pining away for an ambitious CEO, ask yourself if you're comfortable with the idea of two breadwinners outsourcing motherhood to paid alloparents, such as a nanny or daycare. I also highly suggest you look for a more caregiving, nurturing kind of man who can help you balance your career and home life. We'll talk more about this in the next chapter on types of men.

There's no one right way to balance motherhood and career. Mothers who work too much feel guilty about not giving enough time to their kids, and mothers who feel compelled to attend to their kids feel guilty that they're letting down their bosses or not making enough money. Both kinds of mothers envy each other.

One study published by the American Psychological Association found that mothers with jobs report higher levels of happiness than mothers who stay home during their children's infancy and preschool years,[5] but I suspect that the isolation and identity crises of women who aren't prepared for motherhood are big factors.

And now that I've told you that working mothers report higher levels of happiness, the *Journal of Child Development* reports that the more years a mother works, the higher body mass index her kid has.[6] Yep, when we must depend on a village to feed our kids and they're serving fast food for lunch, our children's risk for obesity goes way up. Full-time working mothers have little time to lovingly prepare family meals that are Martha Stewart–worthy.

Want to Be a Single Mother?

Single motherhood may seem like an attractive choice for women who want to have children without the stress of finding the "right" mate, especially for those who earn a high salary and have a wide support system. But there are obvious (and not-so-obvious) concerns. You're ready to make a plan to be a single mother when you can answer "Yes" to the following questions:

1. Have I clearly decided between sperm donation or using the sperm of someone I know?

2. If it's someone I know, have I let go of any fantasy that he'll participate in parenting?

3. Do I make enough money to afford the $18,000 to $35,000 after-tax in annual childcare costs?

4. Do I make enough money to afford life insurance and health insurance?

5. Do I live in a neighborhood with good public schools to save the extra $15,000 to $30,000 a year I would need for private schools?

6. Do I have supportive extended family near me?

7. Am I in a circle of friends who are raising children and will be part of my village?

8. Is my job secure enough to sustain me through any pregnancy complications or an extended maternity leave if my baby has birth issues?

To Cohabitate or to Marry?

Moving in with your boyfriend may seem like a good idea—partly because it's so common today and plenty of people still think it test-drives your relationship before marriage. But in fact it seems to do the opposite. Living together eats up the years of sexual heat and romantic love, and when your relationship settles down to something a little more boring, you're less motivated to tie the knot.

True, cohabitating boyfriends tend to do more housework than husbands do.[7] Married women do seven more hours a week of housework than do live-in girlfriends.[8] And men and women enter living-together relationships for similar positive reasons. They like each other and want to spend time together. They can share expenses, and they think they can explore whether they're compatible for marriage. But the drawbacks of living together play out very differently for men and women. In a research study published in the *Journal of Family Issues*, cohabitating men reported stress over their loss of sexual freedom and women reported worry about the delays in marriage.[9] For women, living with a boyfriend can mean putting marriage and motherhood on a worrisome pause.

And if children do show up while two unmarried people are living together—which is the choice I made—the statistical news isn't great. Children born into cohabiting households don't do as well socially, educationally, and psychologically as kids living in intact married households. The National Marriage Project suggested that these dismal outcomes are related to the instability of living arrangements. Cohabitating couples are more than twice as likely as married couples to break up before the child turns 12. And then what often follows is a rotating crop of adult figures as single parents play musical chairs with boyfriends and girlfriends. That frequent transition of parental figures is linked to poor grades, bad behaviors, drug use, and depression in kids.[10] This startling research is one of the reasons I'm still single after seven years as a single mother. Maintaining stability in my children's lives is paramount for me, and I don't want my kids to see a revolving door of men. (You'll hear more about this in Chapter 10.)

Remember, we're living in an era of relationship transition. Someday, perhaps, we'll have true gender equality and our society will provide the support systems for family so marriage will be less necessary—and less hazardous to navigate. But today, the statistics are still clear. Married couples have better levels of health, wealth, and happiness and their children do better.[11]

No matter how well intentioned, living together increases the chances you won't get married and that you'll divorce if you do. One Swedish study showed that women who lived with their boyfriends before marriage had an 80 percent divorce rate.[12] And here in America, a study in the *Journal of Marriage and Family* found that serial cohabitors are less likely to marry at all. The more often you simply move in with someone, the more you reduce your chances of walking down an aisle. And if a serial cohabitor does marry, she has a much higher divorce rate than someone who previously lived with only one boyfriend.[13]

There's an obvious explanation for this that lies in the psychology of cohabitors. People who choose to live together first tend to be afraid of commitment. They're ambivalent about marriage for a host of reasons, but the number one reason quoted by people who live together is that they're afraid of divorce.[14] This is ironic because living together is one of the biggest factors that contribute to divorce.

The Stay-Over Relationship

There's a new hybrid relationship cropping up all over America. It's called the *stay-over relationship*. It involves two people maintaining two houses but keeping toothbrushes and essentials at both houses. They may sleep at each other's place a few nights a week and may even take a break once in a while to crash at home alone. This kind of relationship is particularly popular with college students or single parents of high school and college students who are free to sleep away but still maintain two solid nests.[15]

Gale, a 41-year-old book publisher, married her love of eight years but still maintains her own home. She and her husband each have daughters from previous marriages in high school and want to keep home life stable for their girls until they head off to college. So, why did they marry? According to Gale: "I was tired of being a divorced single mother. And he was tired of being a divorced single dad. We also felt too old and too committed to be calling each other boyfriend and girlfriend, but we didn't really want to disrupt the lives of our teens with a blended family nor burden our marriage with the challenges of coparenting. So, we live apart."

There's little research on the longevity of stay-over relationships because the trend is just starting to be identified by social scientists. It's thought that stay-over relationships appeal to people who want an intimate relationship but also want a high degree of personal freedom.

"As soon as couples live together, it becomes more difficult to break up," writes Tyler Jamison, doctoral candidate and researcher who identified the trend in a groundbreaking University of Missouri study.[16] "At that point, they have probably signed a lease, bought a couch, and maybe acquired a dog, making it harder to disentangle their lives should they break up. Staying over doesn't present those entanglements." The study found that couples are relatively happy in stay-over relationships but don't necessarily plan to move in together or get married.

While Gale's arrangement seems to be the best of both worlds for her blended family, my instinct is that stay-over relationships without marriage probably have even worse long-term outcomes than cohabitating relationships because they indicate even less of a commitment. Stay-over couples can't even commit to one apartment lease, let alone each other's lifetime.

Divorce-Proof Your Relationship Plan

As I mentioned, the number one reason couples choose to live together and not marry is a fear of divorce. Fears of divorce also fuel our dating addiction, as men and women attempt to prevent a future divorce by either shopping far and wide for the "perfect" partner or by making sure they sow their wild oats before they make a commitment to settle down. I'll explain in the next chapter why both these practices actually increase your chances of breaking up.

We've all heard that the divorce rate hovers around 50 percent. But there are huge numbers of people whose risk of divorce is much lower due to a range of social factors.

If you can answer "Yes" to these questions, there's a strong chance your first-time marriage will stand the test of time:

1. Your first-time marriage happens when you're 25 or older.
2. You and your husband have a bachelor degree or higher.
3. Neither partner has lived with more than one previous partner.
4. You and your partner are strongly religious and practice the same faith.

The Best Laid Plans of Wives and Men

Robert Burns's poetic wisdom "The best laid plans of mice and men often go awry" was later so well paraphrased by John Lennon: "Life is what happens to you while you're busy making other plans."

Of course, life will take its turns. Your relationship life plan will shift and reshape as you age and mature and face different forks in the road. You may meet a caring man when you're only 23 and make an educated decision to marry young. You may experience infertility in your twenties instead of your late thirties and have to revise your relationship plan long before you thought it would be necessary. You may turn 38 and decide to become a single mother if there's no partner in sight. My point is, we can only control our best laid plans so much.

But if we sail through life with no plan at all, trusting the forces of nature and pure luck, we drastically reduce our chances of finding a long-term love that will enable a strong, healthy family unit. This is especially important since we're in a high-supply sexual economy with so much competition for so few peer mates. We need to start somewhere, walking down some road or following some kind of map, or we'll be lost in the forest of love addiction and heartbreak.

The data are strong that marriage and committed romantic relationships improve our health. And strong bonds also improve our emotional states, helping us feel calm, creative, and secure. Research demonstrates that single people are more vulnerable to psychological stress and that good long-term relationships can act as a buffer against all kinds of stress.[17]

Marriage may not be for everyone, but at this turning point in our culture, it's still one of the best choices a woman can make for her health and for her offspring. Please be assured, my advice doesn't come from a place of faith-based beliefs or politically conservative "family values." It comes from sound sociological research.

The tsunami of life may crash upon us while we're busy making other plans, but it helps if we're already standing on higher ground. In the next chapter, I'm going to teach you a little bit about male psychology and explain the wide range of men who are available to you. After that, we're going to talk seriously about sex. That's when we'll begin the detox. It's an age-old technique to eliminate inappropriate men and make the commitment-oriented guys shine before you. I'll also do a little psychological handholding. *The 30-Day Love Detox* may not be an easy transition for you, but I'll give you helpful tools and tips for laying the foundation for a healthy relationship.

Onward, ladies. Your great mate is waiting.

CHAPTER 5

Men: Vampires, Metros, and Superheroes

"**I** play in a band. It's just a garage band, but it's my guy thing. I need it for my manhood," the lanky, blond Norwegian chuckled. We sat in two folding chairs facing the ocean, toes dug in the sand, just chatting. Girlfriends, this is the kind of date many of you will find yourself on in the future. It's called a *play-date,* and we were the supervising parents, idly chatting while two giggling little girls ran around us with pails and shovels.

This guy's wife was a high-powered something-or-other, ensconced in an office tower somewhere, and he was the stay-at-home parent. Our four-year-old girls had met at a summer day camp program and begged us for playdates. So, there we were. Encamped on the beach like a family on vacation. Fortunately, I have excellent boundaries and so did he, and our conversation circled around family, politics, and the weather. It's not always that way. I've been on other playdates with stay-at-home dads that turned downright creepy and flirty.

This is an important point. There are as many kinds of men as there are colors of OPI nail polish. This is true whether they're single, married, or fathers. And to make any sweeping generalization about men is a risky wager.

Anthropologists have long known that human beings have the widest range of paternal investment of any primate. If you saw the 2012 Disneynature movie *Chimpanzee*, you know that the entire movie was based on a freak of nature that the filmmakers happened to capture: an alpha male chimp adopting an orphan baby chimp. This was astonishing, even though chimpanzees and humans share 98 percent of DNA.

Clearly, humans are different. Despite what guys' behavior in bars may suggest, in our evolutionary past, not all hunters had a primary mission of spreading their seed. Plenty stayed home, invented tools, created great cave art, or discovered fire and found their manhood over buffalo steaks on a grill.

Men also have a wide range of sexual behaviors. Some men are born cheaters. Others are biologically or sociologically wired to be monogamous.[1] And there's everything in between.

Men have a range of ambition levels when it comes to creating a family unit and divvying up the responsibilities. Many men are great providers but less skilled at nurturing. While this may work for a traditional one-income family, many working women find themselves feeling resentful when even though they also work full-time, they're always left holding the poopy diaper. This is a perfect example of why relationship planning is so important.

Other men are perfectly content to push the stroller, coach the team, or drive the carpool, but not as likely to bring home a big bonus check. These men are great housekeepers, and many women are adapting to this kind of man today (like the blond Norwegian dad) because they see the value in a great father and homemaker. And these days, a woman can earn enough to support a household. In 40 percent of American families, women are the sole breadwinner.[2] Some women get turned on by this kind of man if only because an involved father is something so many women never had—or perhaps because it enables them to have a successful career and a family. But other women find this kind of man to be downright unsexy and too feminine.

Just look around today to see the vast spectrum of men and their investments in marriage and offspring. It's key to identify who you are first and then take a close look at the pros and cons of potential types of mates.

The Risks/Rewards of a Classic Hunter

Anthropological evidence shows that most women have evolved to be attracted to a specific kind of hunter—the one who would most likely ensure the survival of their offspring either because of his own genetic potential or his ability to bring in protein. Research shows that most women will sit up a little straighter when a tall, muscular, deep-voiced, wealthy man walks in the room.[3] If he also exhibits kindness and intelligence, she may become *his* stalker.[4] Today, look outside any NBA or NFL locker room after a game to see the lineup of short skirts and high heels. Those are cavewoman impulses in action.

That might have been our cavewoman's choice of a good provider and protector, but today's hunky hunter is in a new arena. In today's crowded forests (college campuses, workplaces, Facebook walls), alpha men have so much sexual opportunity that many stray from their nest, even if they didn't inherit cheating DNA. Think professional athletes, famous actors, and successful politicians—and, well, any dude with an extra cell phone and access to a computer.

When I shared this news with a young fashion designer, her face dropped. "But we all want to marry the CEO. We don't want a weak man," she said.

She's talking about what sociologists refer to as the George Clooney Effect. Researchers from the University of Abertay Dundee in Scotland surveyed nearly 4,000 heterosexual men and women and found results that show that the more educated and high earning a woman is, the more likely she is to hold out for a good-looking, older man.[5] The researchers speculate that earning more money makes women lose their instinct for material stability and relationship security, opting instead to go for looks and older age. But as a woman's fertility window closes, those older, good-looking men are more likely to choose a younger woman who seems more fertile. This is the reality so many women ignore.

The Alpha Cheater

Women of all ages are wired to want an alpha male, but in this high-supply sexual economy, single women who want a monogamous relationship also need to think about statistical probability. Commitment-oriented alpha men represent about 0.0001 percent of the male population (I made up that number), and they were probably already snapped up in high school. By the way, if you *are* in high school or college and are dating the football quarterback who fits this description, be aware that infidelity will likely be in his future if he's not tempered with religious programming or self-control that comes from high education. I once sat in on a conversation with four male TV producers who all thought Tiger Woods had a "right to cheat" just because of all the sexual opportunity available to him. It's like male culture endorses a different set of rules for alpha males.

If you can tolerate this and the trade-off of fame and financial security works for you, then more power to you. I'm not judging here; I'm just saying be aware. Most wives of politicians, actors, and pro athletes know the risks and rewards of marrying that kind of hunter. Or they live in denial until one day, they get a reality check and take a golf club to his car windows.

The Five Dominant Man Traits

I'm going to verge from science here for a moment and speak from female wisdom. I have had a long life of observing and interrelating with men. Although I said there are as many different kinds of men as OPI nail polish, there is also a wide range of traits and behaviors in each individual man. And I think many women hold a fantasy that their future mate must be perfectly balanced. He'll be a best friend, a high earner, a sexual athlete, and a good housekeeper. But this is an unrealistic goal that might keep you single.

The truth is, a good provider may not be a good nurturer. A great thinker may be a sloppy housemate. A caregiver may not be a good wage earner. And a Mr. Fix It may not be your best-looking evening arm piece. Just like you, every man you date is a unique snowflake.

That being said, I do believe that in terms of a woman's needs in a relationship, there are five general male traits; whichever one dominates your man's psychology will have a huge impact on your future. Each man tends to lean toward one of these areas, but none of them is the whole package. The first thing to consider when defining your target mate is which dominant trait you would choose if you could have only one.

1. THE PROVIDER

We all know the provider. He's your seatmate in business class staring at spreadsheets for five hours. His bible is the *Wall Street Journal*. He'll hold a stable job and strive to maintain an upscale lifestyle. Because this dude's primary goal in life is to make money, you'll benefit too. (But if he really understands his commitment to you and the family, he won't make you sign a prenuptial agreement. Selfish providers are bad bets.) The downside: Spending so much time at the office makes it hard to be an involved husband and father. Don't count on a provider to put away his BlackBerry on vacation.

2. THE FIXER

This is the guy's guy. He fixes up old cars. He tinkers in the garage on weekends. He wouldn't think of calling a repairman for anything. He's stable and loyal and comfortably middle class. This guy probably won't be your high-class arm piece at social functions, and you may end up making more money than him (although this may work just fine for some women). And he may not be the tidiest, so be prepared to take on most of the housekeeping duties. It's okay. You'll save money on repairmen! And he'll show your kids how to seriously play ball.

3. THE THINKER

If you get turned on by brainiacs, this guy's for you. He's well read, well versed, and, well, seriously book smart. He'll be happy to read the *New York Times* in bed with you on Sunday mornings and loves to listen to NPR and BBC Worldwide on satellite radio. As for earning potential, if he has enough high-functioning habits to overcome the nerd factor, he'll be a good financial partner and a thoughtful planner. He may not be a good dancer, hip dresser, or sports fan. But he's a great conversationalist, always curious, and will be majorly involved in your kids' homework. As far as homemaking goes, it depends on how his mother trained him. Be prepared for his closet to look eerily similar to the shelves of khakis at the Gap.

4. THE CAREGIVER

Caregivers listen to our problems. They help out with homemaking. They can be great cooks and even volunteer to clean up afterward. When we're sick or PMSing, they're at the ready with kindness rather than frustration. They might be nurses, physician's assistants, or paramedics, or they may cover up their nurturing side with a suit every morning. These guys tend to be committed husbands and very involved fathers. But don't plan on a life of luxury: Caregivers' priorities aren't mansions and vacation homes—

unless you plan on buying him one. Some women have trouble with caregivers because they interpret their behavior as too feminine and not attractive. (My two cents: See it as strength!)

5. THE METROSEXUAL

This is the man who'll get a mani-pedi and a spray-on tan with you. He loves his clothes and is as shoe crazy as you. His apartment looks like it sprung from the pages of *Elle Decor*. This guy is great at any social function. Savvy, hip, and fun. However, his priorities may be a little superficial, and he may lose his mind when the baby barfs on his Armani jacket. His focus on appearance can be a turnoff for many women, who perceive this "peacocking" behavior as unmanly. And there's always the fight for mirror time. Also, plan on calling someone else to kill the spider or plunge the toilet.

About That Caring Dude

His arm was burly and warm. As I sat beside him, he elbowed me more than once as he readjusted his tripod and video camera. We were strangers in the bleachers at our children's cheerleading competition. Curious about this super-daddy alpha male hunk, I made small talk and then wormed my way into big talk.

He was on his second marriage. He had two children of his own and had married a single mother with two kids. (Score one for the big guy!) Then, they had a child together. That's five kids. And because they loved kids and family so much, they adopted a sixth child from China. (Another point.) The little angel was sitting beside him in pink glitter and a cheerleading skirt.

"So, who are you videotaping?" I asked. He sighed and shot me a sheepish look.

"Our family loves to be helpful. That's kind of our thing. So, one day, at my oldest daughter's cheering practice, they were short one base [athletes at the bottom of the pyramid] and my son stepped in just to help out. Well, he liked it so much, he joined the team. His team is up next."

Three big points. This guy wasn't gender biased either. Big, tall, handsome, in his late thirties—a rare specimen. I used my simple schema of male psychology and took a chance.

"Let me guess," I asked. "You're a firefighter?"

He looked surprised and wondered how I knew that. I don't profess to know all men. But I know basic schemas. Genuinely nice guys like him tend to gravitate toward caregiving professions. And athletic alpha caregivers end up as firefighters or search and rescue paramedics.

My point is this: Don't turn down a nurturing dude because you think he's weak. Plenty of men who are caring are still very, very masculine.

By the way, his pretty wife returned to the bleachers during our conversation. To say her body language expressed protection was an understatement. If looks could kill! She clearly knows how to keep a good thing in her household.

But the educated, moneymaking women I interviewed for this book seemed averse to sweet, kind men.

"Nice guys are too weak. I hate weak in a man," said a 28-year-old PR executive. The other single women in my wine-and-cheese focus group murmured in agreement. I know too well the feelings of these women. I used to have them myself. The illusion that difficult, challenging men are strong and attractive. That caring, attentive men are weak and not sexy. I wonder what this says about how we value ourselves if we find kindness unattractive. Is this what we think we deserve?

This realization sunk in as I sat in the garden of a girlfriend one night. Her husband rustled up the barbecue, poured me a glass of wine, and attended to the kids while she blow-dried her hair upstairs before her other guests arrived. My guy, by the way, was late as usual, so I had to wrestle with our two kids and drive myself. Yes, like the firefighter's wife, my friend had made a smart choice.

How Men Fall in Love

Within all the basic schemas of men I described earlier are a wide range of fathering styles and commitment levels to a relationship. The good news is this: Seventy-seven percent of U.S. men rate being a good father as very important to them, while only 49 percent gave the same nod to having a successful career.[6] Yep, most men value fatherhood over their careers.

And in an unexpected reversal of gender predictions, another study from Duke Medical Center of more than 200 college students showed that men were more likely than women to praise the value of romantic relationships. The participants were asked to choose among education, career, travel, and a relationship, and more men chose love than did women. The researchers speculate that the results indicate modern women are focused on education and see romance as getting in the way of that.[7] But I think women garner valuable emotional support from female relationships that men often can't obtain from friendships with other men. In short, healthy men need loving women.

But men fall in love in very different ways than women do. First of all, women fall in love faster. And if they're having sex with a man, the rush of oxytocin will increase the chances that a woman perceives a frequent sexual relationship as a growing love relationship.

Men don't think like that. To men, sex and love are two distinct concepts. Granted, men can have intimate sex with a woman they love, and many report that the sex is better when they have an emotional connection. But men can also have regular, exciting, vigorous sex with the same woman over a long period of time and never fall in love with her. Remember the smash comedy *Bridesmaids* and poor Kirsten Wiig's "f—k buddy"? She was in love, but he sure wasn't.

Men who can fall in love and become securely attached for the long term (more than half of American men) more often associate feelings of trust with feelings of love. When a man feels a woman is his undeniable supporter and trustworthy confidante, he can begin to have deeper feelings for her. And there's a timing thing that women don't always have.

Women fall in love when they feel they've met the right man. Men fall in love when they reach their state of readiness. That state of readiness can be influenced by a number of factors: his age, his income, his job security, the coupling trend of his peer group, and even a family trauma.

Recently, I sat at a dinner party beside a good-looking financial planner and his real estate agent wife. They were newlyweds, and I was curious about why these young people tied the knot in our high-supply sexual culture. He was quick to tell me that his dad had always told him that when he met a woman he could trust, he should grab her and make that commitment.

His mention of his father was only part of the truth. The dinner party hostess told me later that his father had recently passed away and his mother had just been diagnosed with breast cancer. Now if this kind of loss of one's secure attachment figures isn't enough to make anyone create a new support system, I don't know what is.

The biggest point here is that you may be the perfect girlfriend or wife for a guy, but if he hasn't reached his state of readiness, he won't step up to the plate. As one man who runs counseling groups for men explained to me: "Once a guy hits his time, he'll swing at whatever girl is up at bat. He may have dated better women before or there may be better women in his future, but when a man is ready to commit, he's ready."

So, looking for a commitment-oriented man is really a matter of looking for a man who's ready. For example, the average age men marry at for the first time is 27. If he's past that age, he's either getting ready or he could be emotionally avoidant. If he's finished school and has a secure job, he's likely ready. If his siblings and friends are married, he's probably getting ready to follow suit. If his parents are still married, there's a good chance he's wired to get there.

All too often, women look at a man's compatibility rather than his state of readiness. They simply don't ask the crucial questions that would reveal if he might be at the right stage of life to commit. A woman tends to assume that if she's ready, he must be. Or she tries to hang out with him for as long as possible, hoping he'll hit that stage. But the wait could be too long.

And, more tragic, even when he clearly tells her he's not ready for a relationship, some women plow ahead anyway with their hearts in their hands, hoping to convince him otherwise. Ladies, pay attention when a man says he's not ready for a relationship, even if he's being kind and spending time and money on you. It means he's happy with the status quo (sex) but nothing more.

Monogamous Men

More great news: Most men not only value love, but they can also be monogamous. A couple years back, huge media attention was paid to a study from the Laboratory of Evolutionary Anthropology and Health at Binghamton University, State University of New York, indicating the presence of a "cheater gene" in as many as four out of ten men. The researchers gathered sexual history data from 181 men and compared it to their DNA.

"What we found was that individuals with a certain variant of the DRD4 gene were more likely to have a history of uncommitted sex, including one-night stands and acts of infidelity," said Justin Garcia, doctoral diversity fellow. "The motivation seems to stem from a system of pleasure and reward, which is where the release of dopamine comes in. In cases of uncommitted sex, the risks are high, the rewards substantial, and the motivation variable—all elements that ensure a dopamine 'rush.'"[8]

If the researchers are correct, an addiction to sex is actually an addiction to dopamine, a neurotransmitter that activates the pleasure center in our brain and releases an abundance of "feel good" chemicals. But those other six out of ten "monogamous" men still like a little dopamine rush. They more likely get it from playing weekend tag football, hang gliding, driving fast cars, skiing, mountain bike riding, a heavy workout at the gym, an exciting and risky business launch, and even taking social risks.

Before you decide that four out of ten men are guaranteed to be sexually unfaithful, consider that the study was done on only 181 men and used self-reported data. That means the guys had to tell the truth about their sexual behavior, and most men enhance the number of conquests when asked about it. I think the jury will be out for a long time about whether the cheater gene exists at all. And my suspicion is, the gene might indicate an attachment disorder more than a sexual one.

The Seven Deadly Signs of a Cheater

It's the thing women worry about the most. In our hunter-gatherer past, if a woman discovered that her man was being unfaithful, she risked that valuable resources would be leaving the hut along with his appendage. It's a visceral, natural female fear closely linked to our survival instinct. A woman left alone with offspring to raise suffers immense hardships—not to mention the emotional damage. Today, not much has changed in that department.

Data are varied about how many married men cheat on their spouses. The *Journal of Couple & Relationship Therapy* published a study in 2002 that reported that about 60 percent of American men cheat on their wives at some point in their marriages. Women cheat too—but still much less often than men.[9]

But there are ways to tell if you're dating a future cheater—and ways to reduce your risks, if you will. In fact, research points to seven factors that increase the chance your boyfriend might become a cheater. If he has five or more, I'd worry:

1. SEXUAL ANXIETY

Believe it or not, the more sexually confident and macho a man is, the less likely he is to cheat. A new study from the

University of Guelph in Canada found that men with sexual performance anxiety are more likely to wander.[10] This may be because they're trying to prove themselves or attempting to determine if a different partner might help their performance. Or perhaps they're simply less embarrassed sexually when there's less emotional connection with a partner.

2. AN AVOIDANT ATTACHMENT STYLE

As we talked about in Chapter 3, some men are unable to have emotional intimacy. They may seek out sexual relationships outside their primary one simply because there's no threat of intimacy. Some men have difficulties having rich, passionate sex with the woman they love yet can easily perform with a stranger. Cheating can even help them avoid commitment because it distances them from their partner and gives them a feeling of freedom.[11]

3. LESS EDUCATION

Men with higher education and higher IQs are less likely to cheat. Remember, for some men, monogamy requires an intellectual decision. And the more intelligent, the better equipped they are to stay mentally strong.[12] HLN's Dr. Drew, the host of *Loveline,* calls this the "muscles of monogamy."

4. NO RELIGIOUS OBSERVANCE

Besides intelligence, one of the most powerful enforcers of monogamy is religion.[13] Most religions teach a kind of family value. Loyalty and respect to the mother of their children is woven into the teachings of just about every religion in the world.

5. HE MAKES WAY MORE MONEY THAN YOU DO

Research shows that powerful men are likely to cheat.[14] This may be because wealthy men have more opportunity for sexual affairs, and it may also be that the personality of a driven, ambitious man makes him require continual proof that he's powerful. It's actually an insecurity that fuels his

Five Signs He's a Bad Boy

1. He has a string of angry ex-girlfriends.
If your date is always telling you stories about crazy ex-girlfriends and prior stormy relationships, run. He's clearly telling you he breaks women's hearts and doesn't have good conflict-resolution skills.

2. He doesn't feel much guilt.
Does guilt motivate his behavior? Is he comfortable bending the rules at work, even if it might hurt a coworker? Does he cheat on his tax returns? Does he tell too many "white" lies? Then he's probably lying to you, too.

3. He fears emotional intimacy.
Most men fear emotional intimacy more than most women do. But bad boys have multiple lovers so they can avoid all real intimacy. If he's not getting real and vulnerable with you, he's likely a bad boy.

4. He drives a flashy car and spends money on a first date.
Bad boys know the weapons needed to have short-term relationships: Look rich even if you aren't. Good guys are more likely to live within their means and take you on great experiences rather than buy you things early on.

5. He wants things to be perfect.
Bad boys often have a distorted belief that relationships should be perfect and that arguments and disappointments are unacceptable. He's more likely to cheat in retaliation or dump a woman because he's looking for perfection.

need for wealth. (By the way, economic dependency has the opposite effect on women.[15] When they depend on a man for resources, women are smart enough not to mess with the gravy train.)

6. HE EARNS LESS THAN YOU DO

As you read in the first chapter of this book, research shows that when men are economically dependent on women, they're more likely to cheat.[16] This is thought to be related to a need to assert themselves when their strong male-provider identity is threatened.

7. HE SHOWS LITTLE EMPATHY

A Spanish study revealed that the interpersonal sensitivity (empathy) of men is lower compared with that of women. This could affect their ability to empathize with their partner's feelings of betrayal, making them more likely to have affairs. This study that found that men feel less guilt than women also showed that this difference is particularly stark in the 40- to 50-year-old age group—one particularly vulnerable to the midlife crisis affair.[17]

Can a Tiger Change His Stripes?

We've all wondered whether a former cheater can change, and we come up with lots of reasons to think his behavior would be totally different with us as the "perfect" girlfriend. The truth is that the more sexual partners he has had in the past—combined with the more cheating episodes (and he'll likely downplay that number)—the less likely he is to transform. Our bodies are amazing machines we can train for anything. But if he's addicted to the dopamine rush that comes with frequent sexual partners and infidelity, it's really hard to change. Would you date a meth addict hoping he's going to eventually clean up?

That being said, there are a couple of biological events that can affect a man's testosterone level. And that may lead to changes in sexual behavior. For example, during the third trimester of his wife's pregnancy, a husband's testosterone level begins to decline. It makes a steep drop right after the birth of the baby. Anthropologists speculate this supplies evolutionary advantage by diverting sexual energy away and encouraging more nurturing behaviors. This study, conducted at Northwestern University, indicates that a man's biology can change substantially to help meet the demands of fatherhood. This could explain why single men often have poorer health than married men and fathers. "If fathers have lower testosterone levels, this might protect them against certain chronic diseases as they age," researcher Christopher Kuzawa, PhD, said.[18]

Another study shows that men have reduced incidences of risky behavior—crime, drugs, tobacco—after the birth of their first child.[19] Parenthood is a transformative experience for both genders. And men get many benefits. But as for curing a philanderer? That's gotta be up to him, and there's not a lot you can do to influence that.

Why We Love Bad Boys

If 100 men ages 18 to 23 go out on a first date tonight, how many will have enough of an "A" game to obtain sex from a woman? I was shocked in one of my wine-and-cheese focus groups that some women thought it would be as high as

80 percent! In actuality, one study showed that the number is more like 20.[20] That's one in five. Every night, 20 percent of men we don't know well—who wouldn't be trusted with the keys to our house to water our plants—are given access to our bloodstreams and our eggs on a first date.

Thankfully, 80 percent of women are too smart to engage in high-risk first-date sex. But the only explanation I can give for the rest is that they're misinformed about the risks. Health risks aside, the risk of disappointment and a broken heart after first-date sex is astronomical.

But rather than blaming women, let's take a look at these guys who master short-term sexual strategies. The answer is what we colloquially call *bad boys*. We feel good in their presence because they may be gorgeous, fun, often rich, and full of personality. Or they may be tortured, creative, and brooding and arouse our caregiving instincts. They may compliment us. They may sweetly insult us. They may show up late. They may not call for weeks. But we get addicted to them.

There are three main reasons why some women are particularly susceptible to the allure of a bad boy. First, it may be their own anxious attachment style. Women who crave intimacy often invite the very thing they fear: a man who'll abandon them at a crucial moment of need. Sadly, about one in three American women suffered abuse during childhood,[21] and whether that abuse was physical, sexual, or emotional, it most likely came at the hand of someone they loved.[22] These girls grow up to believe that mistreatment is normal or, at the very least, that they have the skills to survive it. Happiness and proper care may be absolutely foreign to some women, and they're terrified by it.

The second reason why some women are attracted to bad boys is they confuse his emotional unavailability with self-confidence and a higher status. Getting a bad boy to commit would be a huge accomplishment—a major boost to a woman's self-worth. Many women pursue bad boys in an attempt to change and conquer one. Instead, with each rejection, they're continually reminded about their perceived unworthiness.

Finally, bad boys are like a Las Vegas slot machine. They're an exciting chemical high with a mixture of hope, profits, and potential for loss. Both are based on a behavioral learning theory called *random interval reward system*.[23]

Learning theorists, such as Pavlov, Watson, and Skinner, spent their professional lives attempting to figure out what motivates animal and human behavior. One of the things they discovered is that the most effective way to get an organism (that's you!) addicted to a behavior is to administer the reward in a random way. The recipient of the reward doesn't know what's coming or when, but the very fact that it's random and pleasurable glues them to the behavior.

This is the basic principle behind a slot machine. Say you were given a consistent but small reward with every fifth pull of the lever. You would probably quickly become bored and move on. And if the reward was exactly $1 each time, even though it was given at random intervals, you would still eventually become bored.

The secret is the varying size of the reward and varying interval rate. For example, if on the tenth pull you received $200, your brain would have "learned" to survive ten pulls for such an exciting reward. To keep you going, a series of small payoffs might come quickly. In this example, the machine knows you'll continue to deposit money for at least ten pulls if it has rewarded you at least once in that manner. The owners of Vegas casinos calculated all these odds years ago, and they know how to set the random intervals to keep the player addicted to popping in coins. Surprise, surprise—the house always wins.

Bad boys operate the same way. Imagine that every text, phone call, compliment, intimate glance, and touch from a lover is recorded by your brain as a positive reward. Now imagine that it's given in a random way. I like to call this the *bad boy success formula*. It's because a bad boy's fear of emotional intimacy causes him to dash in and out of a woman's life in what feels like a random way. In actuality, his pattern of advance and retreat is a reflection of how much emotional intimacy he can tolerate. But who's looking below the surface when you're busy staring at your phone, wondering why he hasn't called?

Each time a bad boy feels it's safe to return to a woman, his object is usually to obtain physical intimacy. Because sex is his main goal, a bad boy is particularly savvy at coming on with compliments and making you feel like a queen—all rewards that women thrive on. Bad boys

Signs He's Commitment Oriented

1. His parents are still married.
2. He's older than age 27.
3. His peer group is getting married.
4. He's college educated.
5. He's religious.
6. He lives in a so-called red state (politically conservative).
7. He has a secure job.
8. He has had at least one long-term girlfriend (more than a year).
9. He has a good relationship with his mother (but not too close).
10. He refers to you as his girlfriend rather than "the girl I'm dating right now."

are also the very best apologizers. The apology is part of their game to wedge back in your door. Sometimes, their words of contrition resemble a kind of emotional intimacy, so women fall for it again and again.

But now it's time to detox forever on bad boys, commitment phobes, and inappropriate men. The next chapter may very well be the most important chapter in this book and the most important thing you'll ever read about dating and mating. It's a clear behavioral prescription to help you take back control of your love life. Your feminine power starts now!

CHAPTER 6

The 30–Day Love Detox

A 29-year-old TV producer smiled at me as she summed up the belief system of so many women today: "We are controllers. We can control our education and we can control our careers, but we can't control men."

She's right: Women can't control men. But women can control themselves long enough to ascertain if a man is a low-risk partner. And that's the basis for *The 30-Day Love Detox*. Using the detox will allow you to shed the bad guys and get the good guys to pursue you harder so you know whom to invest in. It's that simple.

The New Courting Rituals

Let me make this clear: *The 30-Day Love Detox* isn't an old-fashioned "withholding of sex" in order to manipulate a guy or to make him fall in love with you. *The 30-Day Love Detox* is about awarding yourself the space to evaluate him. It's giving him an opportunity to become a beautiful male peacock who displays his feathers and invents some new courting rituals to woo you.

Sociologist Anthony Paik, PhD, who teaches gender studies and sexuality at the University of Iowa, says that old forms of courtship may not seem hip today, but they were valuable. "There is a lot of confusion. Things are muddled. People know what is effective historically, but they are no longer doing it. People are rejecting the old traditions of courtship because they may seem staid, and there are likely good reasons for moving beyond old rituals. But what's getting lost is the information that came with those traditions."

In the old courting traditions, if a guy sacrificed a lot of time, energy, and money, he was probably looking for a long-term relationship. One Chicago college student laughed as she illustrated that pattern to me: "I swear, I had a dozen expensive dates with one guy, and I never had sex with him. I tried to like him. I really did. This guy was good boyfriend material for someone—just not me."

Sadly, most women can't wait this long to see a man's intentions. In our postmodern culture, the rise of women has caused many people to reject the old traditions.

"But we haven't replaced them with new ones," says Dr. Paik. "And it then becomes more difficult to scrutinize people's intentions about their willingness to build long-term relationships. The loss of some old traditions is, in a way, a loss of information. It doesn't mean that we must return to traditional courtship. We can have new rituals— even idiosyncratic ones that provide this information. The key is that we must have something that acts as a credible signal of people's intentions."

The 30-Day Love Detox is a way to set up some new rituals and create space for men to display their intentions. Modern men may not signal their intentions with such traditional sacrifices as expensive flowers and candlelit restaurants, but they'll find new ways to tell you you're important. A potential commitment-oriented guy may respond to you kindly—and publicly—on your Facebook wall, or he might call you when he'd prefer to text. He might take the time to meet you before an event rather than have you meet him there. He might pick up his cell phone when he's with other people and call you by name rather than simply say "Hey."

You two will have time—because your focus isn't on sex—to talk about your families, your careers, and your life goals. You'll find when you sit across from him in a restaurant that there are so many things to say when your mouth isn't provocatively sucking on a chocolate-covered strawberry and he isn't licking his lips. Taking early sex off the table clears the clouds. It gives you perspective to make a smart, informed decision.

Men Know What's Up

When I want to know something about men and their habits, I go to the source. I ask a man. I'm a little suspicious of uber-educated female "experts" who have spent more time in women's studies departments than in men's clubs. One such researcher responded to my question about new courtship rituals like this: "Why should women care about men's intentions? If he's good in bed, have him stay a few days and see if he takes the trash out."

She missed the point. Most of the women I interviewed can barely get a guy to stay until sunrise, let alone a few days or a lifetime. Certainly, some women are happy to become more like men, and some of them invented the *Sex and the City* culture by erroneously assuming men and women have the same kind of sexuality. But I believe that author Alice B. Sheldon, who wrote science fiction in the 1960s and 1970s under a male pseudonym, got it right when she said: "There are only two genders. Men and Mothers."[1]

Women and men can be on equal footing in almost all aspects of life—until motherhood rears its exceptional head. Men don't birth babies, they don't breastfeed, and many of them aren't wired to nurture in the same way most women are. And no matter how many progressive stay-at-home dads are out there, most men just aren't lining up in droves to take that job. In fact, there were recent complaints about the gender-neutral family leave policy at the Massachusetts Institute of Technology that said fathers could opt to take paternity leave so their partners could get back to work fast. The complaints were from working mothers who said the fathers used most of their "paternity" time taking on extra work projects and building their careers in other ways while their wives worked and came home to a messy house.[2]

Thus, I admit: The idea for *The 30-Day Love Detox* came from a man—one who loves to text multiple women at a time and have plenty of noncommitted sex. Women grovel after him because he's whip smart and emotionally unavailable. I found myself attracted to him even as I interviewed him for this book.

"If women could just hold off for thirty days, they would eliminate 90 percent of the male static in their lives," said the playboy (who would never consider doing such a thing himself). "But women need a wide bandwidth of male attention, so they're too afraid to try it."

There it was. Lightbulb time. A big, bright halogen lightbulb that almost gave me a headache. The high-supply sexual economy hurts women. It may make us feel temporarily liberated, but it sets us up for relationship failure in the long run.

Most of the progressive and independent women I interviewed for this book felt that their own orgasms were enough of an exchange for sex. They were more likely to dump a prospective boyfriend because he had a substandard penis rather than because he had a substandard heart. If only they knew that this kind of thinking is robbing them of the freedom to find a truly satisfying relationship.

That's when I decided: Women need a love purge. A detox. We need to clear away the clouds of alcohol, sex hormones, and tech addiction. We need to see men more clearly. And we need remedies for all our withdrawal symptoms. Then, we can reintroduce love to our diets—that is, men with high emotional nutrition. This is how we'll take back control of our relationships.

The Five Sexual Myths That Keep Women Single

If you've gotten this far in the book, you know a few things about yourself. You know who you are, if your attachment style makes you susceptible to bad boy addictions, if you're comfortable with nontraditional gender roles, if you can financially or biologically afford to wait for motherhood, or if you should get on this right now. You also know a few things about men, such as which kind have a low likelihood of commitment.

But before I give you the complete prescription, I need

to bust a few sexual myths that are being passed around our culture. These five myths are so pervasive that many people will argue that they're God-spoken truth. I used to believe a few of them myself until I interviewed some of the brightest minds in the country who focus on sexuality, mating strategies, and attachment. Even I had to take a deep breath and let go of some of my cherished arguments for sexual equality when I saw how solidly the research ran contrary to my beliefs. Trust me, ladies, these are the myths that will keep you single if you continue to believe them.

1. THE HOOKUP CULTURE IS EVERYWHERE

As I mentioned earlier, the hookup culture is more urban legend than reality. A recent National Survey of Family Growth study with more than 13,000 participants showed that fully one-quarter of college students are virgins.[3] But most people assume that college campuses are a hotbed of noncommitted sex. And they believe this uncommitted sex happens earlier than it does.[4] In fact, young adults who don't attend college have more sexual partners.[5]

But because the perceptions exist, many women feel subtly pressured to have sex before they're ready. One study showed that the vast majority of college students talked about hookups yet reported very few actual sexual scores. But the talk was the damaging part for women. It has the effect of "normalizing" the practice and creating more approval for hookups. That new false norm causes many women to engage in risky sexual behavior.[6]

The truth is there are two distinct dating markets. One sells bulk sex at a low price—perhaps the price of one drink or a cleverly worded text—and the other sells a select variety to a narrow market. Women who want a healthy relationship "charge" a high price for sex: attention, love, care, commitment, and social status. In today's times, social status may not mean marriage, but it can certainly mean he changes his Facebook status to indicate he's in a relationship with you.

2. SEXUAL CHEMISTRY HELPS RELATIONSHIPS

Many women believe that jumping into bed in the early stages of a relationship is a way to test sexual compatibility—a way to audition a man, if you will. Someone (probably a man) created the myth that "sexual chemistry" is necessary before couples can move to a committed relationship. If this theory were true, then people who don't test sexual chemistry before commitment should have shorter, less happy relationships. But psychology professor Dean Busby, PhD, and his colleagues at Brigham Young University were unable to make this connection in a study of more than 2,000 couples. People with good sexual chemistry early on didn't stay together longer. He explained his results to me this way: "The mechanics of good sex are not particularly difficult or beyond the reach of most couples, but the emotions, the vulnerability, the meaning of sex, and whether it brings couples closer together are much more complicated to figure out."

"Sexual chemistry isn't made by some effortless match, as if the couple won a lottery," says University of Texas at Austin sociology professor Mark Regnerus, PhD, author of *Premarital Sex in America: How Young Americans Meet, Mate, and Think about Marrying.* "I think sexual chemistry is the title we give to the erotic novelty often found in early sexual relationships: If they're 'hot,' then chemistry must exist. But all relationships settle down into more sustainable patterns of romance, and *that* is when sexual chemistry is fashioned."

3. PEOPLE HAVE SEXUAL "NEEDS"

Sex researchers have long known that women have different kinds of sexual "needs" than men. Women's sexuality tends to be responsive, meaning we respond to sexual opportunity rather than seek it out to fulfill some kind of necessary quota.[7] When women meet someone they're attracted to, their sexual responses turn on. When we break up from a sexual relationship, we aren't as likely as men to replace that relationship with daily masturbation or pornography.

When single women feel "horny," it's often an extension of their emotional need for companionship. Some researchers have found that women often desire to be desired.[8] That's a whole lot different from a biological desire for sex— any sex—with almost anyone. Men are more like that. This model of female sexuality is supported by the fact that drug companies can't come up with a drug that enhances female libido. Women's sexuality is a complicated mix of psychology, social conditioning, and biology. Men's sexuality is closer to basic plumbing.

But in this high-supply sexual economy where women have adopted everything male, I often hear women say: "But what about my sexual needs? I have to put my needs aside?"

I believe the bodies of those women could be responding to our highly sexualized culture, including provocative advertising, half-naked men on Facebook, and sexual invitations at every turn, making women believe that sex is urgent. Rather than having a sexual response to a single suitor they're attracted to, women could be having a sexual response to our crazy sexualized environment. Or they could simply be parroting men. Worse, they could be giving in to the power wielded by the shrinking supply of good men and bowing to their requests out of fear.

These women believe the myth that sex is in fact a *human* need. Granted, psychologist Abraham Maslow's famous hierarchy of human needs puts sex at the base of the pyramid—right alongside pooping—but he isn't referring to sex as a commodity.[9] He was referring to sexual competition as a motivating factor for people's behaviors. And I think it's clear we have enough sexual competition these days.

Can both genders control their sexuality? Of course we can! Sex is no more a need than a trip to Saks Fifth Avenue. For our human survival, we *need* air, food, water, shelter, and companionship. Ask any priest, nun, military person stationed abroad, prisoner, or elderly widow. Is sex necessary for their survival? Nope. But it's a nice perk that comes with freedom, prosperity, and good health.

I think the important question women need to ask themselves is this: Does more sex make a woman feel liberated or trapped? I vote for trapped. By adopting a male model of sexuality, we've imprisoned ourselves in a hookup culture that trained a generation of men to avoid marriage and parental responsibilities. Is this getting our "needs" met?

4. SEX LEADS TO LOVE

While slightly more than half of college women believe a sexual hookup can be a stepping-stone to a relationship, the research points to a more ominous outcome. According to Dr. Regnerus: "It's a race to the bottom. Having sex early in a relationship—or, worse, before it even starts—is a guaranteed failure. It's just a matter of time. Men won't sacrifice for someone who's easy. They don't work that way."[10]

Renowned evolutionary psychology professor David Buss, PhD, at the University of Texas at Austin and Martie G. Haselton, PhD, at UCLA found that the greater number of previous sexual partners a man has, the more likely he is to quickly perceive diminished attractiveness in a woman after first intercourse.[11] Sex doesn't lead to love for men. And if the guy is a player, sex more often leads to disdain for you.

My Facebook page, like yours, is crammed with visually wired men who click on any cute photo that might mean a sexual opportunity, thus the majority of my Facebook "friends" are men. When I posted the Buss and Haselton study on my Facebook page, one guy summed it up perfectly: "Sure—it's a test. We see how quick we can get you in bed. The quicker you are, the less wifey material you are." Sigh. Feminism has yet to reprogram men's brains in the area of sexuality.

5. PROMISCUITY CAN BE TURNED OFF

Plenty of people believe that sex is a behavior that's very malleable—that sexuality can be turned on and off like a light switch. Many of the women I spoke with told me they're hooking up as a way to audition mates, but they're quite sure they can be faithful when they decide to be. But research doesn't support this. More likely is the scenario that these women are training their bodies to be future cheaters. We can train ourselves for most anything. And the only way to train for monogamy is to either abstain or be monogamous.

"Many will say, 'When I get ready to settle down, I'm

going to take things more slowly,'" says Dr. Busby, whose work studying thousands of singles and couples has produced relevant and timely data. "Unfortunately, some of our more recent research seems to suggest that the patterns that develop in young adulthood and their relational consequences can't just be turned off or avoided once a person decides it is time to marry. Every relationship we have, however brief and insignificant, influences every other relationship we have, and the patterns that we repeat across relationships become very difficult to change."

Exiting the High–Supply Sexual Marketplace

Here's the rub: You do have mating control, but you're also in a race against your fertility clock and an ever-increasing competition for a narrowing market of good mates. I hope those fears will outweigh any fears you may have of dealing with the aftershock of pulling yourself off the high-supply sexual market. Think of it this way: Even in a bumper tomato crop year, when high supply forces the price of tomatoes down to a nickel a head, there will still be a market for an artisan-grown, organic, heirloom tomato that sells for a dollar. So, which are you? A mass-market, low-priced date? Or a woman whose own intimacy is valuable and worth the price? And the price should be love, care, commitment, and financial partnership.

Before I give you the prescription, I want to assure you that while a male friend may have planted the seed, *The 30-Day Love Detox* was created and fine-tuned by using the advice of a wide range of experts in psychology, anthropology, biology, and sociology.

One study in particular strongly supported the thirty-day rule. Dr. Paik discovered data that indicates that the onset of sex *after* the first month of dating can lead to commitment. "In one of my studies, it turned out that the longer couples delayed sex, the more exclusive the relationship. And if men engage in sex within the first month of dating, they are 4.5 times more likely to be nonexclusive later."[12]

I want to be clear: Waiting thirty days to begin the sexual relationship isn't a magic pill. In fact, the *longer* you wait to have sex, the more you improve your chances of bonding with a good mate. But thirty days does slow the pace enough so you can begin to really pay attention to all his signals—signals that indicate how important you are to him. For example, you might notice he's calling to schedule dates rather than texting you at 11:00 p.m. for sex. This is a signal you'd never have gotten if you hooked up the first night and are happy with only a booty call.

Dr. Regnerus's extensive research on young adults' sexual habits shows that waiting thirty days to have sex for the first time increases the chances you'll still be a couple one year later. Nearly 90 percent of the fast movers in his study had broken up before one year. However, if the couples waited thirty days, 24 percent were still together a year later.[13]

Think about it: Nearly one in four couples were actually couples a year later and for one major reason: They waited a mere month to begin knocking boots. And that number jumped even higher if a couple waited more than thirty days before jumping in the sack. Then, the success rate was one in three. Would you rather have odds that looked like one in ten or one in three? *The 30-Day Love Detox* doesn't guarantee a successful mate in one month, but it does guarantee a higher statistical probability that you'll find and keep a mate.

The 30-Day Love Detox

....

1. Purge all noncommitted men. The first step is to clean out your life of all junk food men so you're ready to meet really great guys. If you'd like to try giving your favorite "friend with benefits" an ultimatum to obtain a commitment, you're welcome to try. Ask him to change his Facebook relationship status and see what happens. Sadly, the statistical probability won't point to a positive result, so brace yourself.

2. No sex! Make a vow not to have sex—no groping, no oral sex, no French kissing, not even grinding with clothes on—for thirty days after meeting a new guy. A handshake and good night kiss on the cheek are all that's allowed. (And no sexting, either. As you'll hear about in Chapter 9 on technology and dating, sexting and naked photos are basically sex to a guy. He's getting almost as much gratification as with a warm body, and all his ingrained notions about the double standard will make him devalue you.)

3. Remain calm and in control. Practice saying "No" without anger or any other information other than a friendly smile. I'll give you some tips on page 142. And do *not* say anything about the love detox! Any guy who knows the deal will wait thirty days to extract sex—with no intention of commitment.

4. Stop drinking if it reduces your resolve. Or at the very least, stick to one glass of wine per date. Alcohol is the number one reason women tell me they have sex when they don't want to. And in Dr. Regnerus's research, he found that one in three women who drink every day reports having sex on the first date. Of those who drink only a couple times a week, only 12 percent reported first-date sex.[14]

5. Look for men who fit your relationship life plan. If his age, his education, or his social class doesn't match your needs, purge him. Research shows that these kinds of clashes most often lead to breakups. Remember: Definitely no junk food men allowed. But start to consider men who may not have the height, hair, race, or high income you had originally hoped for. There may be a pearl in that oyster.

The Advanced Detox

If after thirty days you're still unsure, follow this rule: Don't have sex until he agrees to be sexually exclusive. And make sure he says it—out loud—with clear words. Research shows that most couples make assumptions about monogamy. They don't obtain a verbal contract. And that's how people get hurt.[15]

And there's good news about having higher levels of commitment before beginning a sexual relationship. Sandra Metts, PhD, professor of communication at Illinois State University, headed a study called the Passion Turning Point, in which she looked at which came first for 286 college students: the words "I love you" or sex. Her results are fascinating. If couples made a commitment to be exclusive before they had sex, then their sexual experience became a positive turning point in their relationship. It increased mutual understanding, trust, and sense of security. But when a commitment wasn't obtained before the onset of sex, the sex was more often considered a negative turning point that evoked regret, uncertainty, and discomfort, and prompted apologies.[16] Ouch. Been there, done that.

Why "No" Is a Dirty Word

I've noticed something about women. Many of us have an incredibly hard time saying no. We love to be pleasing and compliant and not make people mad. It's a terrible feeling when people are mad at us. And when we say no, anger is one possible reaction. There are also women who have been conditioned since early childhood to believe that saying no is unkind and selfish. But perhaps the biggest reason some women have trouble saying no is they're afraid to be undesirable. Somehow, our self-esteem is wrapped up in how much we're liked. I'll address how to deal with the withdrawal symptoms that show up when useless men begin to dislike us, but for now, let's focus on the incredible power of the word *no*.

A writer once interviewed me for a women's magazine—you know, the kind that tells you how to dress sexy, act sexy, and please him sexually. The journalist asked me if I thought that women who refused to text would be perceived as "difficult" by men. I responded by saying "Only by difficult men." Good guys rise to the challenge and easily make sacrifices for a good woman. But more disturbing to me about this question was the fact it demonstrated just how much power men have in this mating market.

I've found that we gals have so few skills and so little experience in saying no that plenty of us say yes to sex we don't even want. Some of the researchers I interviewed found that alarming numbers of young women are participating in unwanted sex. They're either doing particular *acts* they don't feel comfortable with or having full-on intercourse with *people* they don't feel comfortable with.[17]

I admit it. Even I have had sex on occasion with someone

who outpressured me. While it wasn't physical pressure that felt threatening, it was psychological pressure. Let's face it: Guys have an answer for everything. And no matter how many reasons you give them for not wanting to have sex with them on that very night, they'll have at least two reasons why having sex with them is an excellent idea. Men are prepared for a pushback. And you've got to be prepared for their courtroom-worthy arguments.

First-Class Negotiators

An attorney friend recently told me about a lavish wedding he had just attended. Lately, whenever I hear about weddings or newlyweds, I'm curious about why and how they made such a commitment in a high-supply sexual economy.

"Who's getting married these days?" I asked him.

"A female lawyer," he laughed. "Those women always know how to negotiate a deal."

I laughed too. But then another lightbulb went off. Sex, love, and commitment are one big negotiation, and

How to Say "No" Successfully

1. Be clear and honest. No wishy-washy language.

2. Use body language. Move away from him.

3. Be vulnerable. Explain that you find saying "No" to be hard.

4. Replace the words "I can't" with "I don't want to."

5. If you're interested in him, put warmth in your voice so as not to appear rude.

6. Don't apologize.

7. Say less, not more. No need to explain why.

men, I've learned, are first-class negotiators when it comes to obtaining sex. That's why *The 30-Day Love Detox* is your ticket to becoming a better relationship negotiator.

The 30-Day Love Detox is about learning to negotiate a healthy relationship. The first part of the negotiation is to win the battle for time so you can make an informed decision. The second part is to win the negotiation for commitment and the third part to win the negotiation for the kind of relationship system you want to live in.

How to Say "No"

There are plenty of ways to politely avoid sex in the early stages of dating. Here are my top four strategies:

1. The quick goodbye. This is the fast peck on the cheek and dash out of his car, skip down the subway platform, or sprint into your apartment building lobby. It gives no time for him to ask, pressure, or negotiate. It's just too quick. Always end it with a smile, a hug, and warm, happy energy. A few minutes after you scram, he'll probably call or text to keep up the chase. Simply send a couple XOs and a smiley face and turn off your phone. You've won that stage of negotiation.

2. The empathetic "No." This one shows that you understand his desire but follows up with an assertive expression about your decision. When his hands start to grope and his lips and tongue try to make their way to your mouth, you might say something like: "I know how this feels—to want something more physical. But I don't want to."

3. The direct "No." The trick here is to keep your energy happy and warm. Keep smiling when you simply say "No." When he asks why, smile harder and say "No" in an even softer, kinder voice. Give no more information. You don't need to.

4. The maybe later "No." This is the tricky one because it involves giving a little information about why you're saying no. You might say something like "Not tonight" or "Not this early in a relationship." This implies he has a big chance another time—and it might make him up the pressure, but it can also be a flirty way to keep his attention.

Did you notice I gave you few words? Good negotiators know that rule number one of any negotiation is to say very little. The more information you give him about why you're saying no, the more targets he has for his psychological pressure. As you start to list your reasons, he'll be a master at finding ways to rationalize your "misguided" decision. Don't give him ammunition or he'll use it against you. He'll put you down. He'll put down this book. He'll put me down. He'll give you false assurances about his intentions. In this high-supply sexual economy, he doesn't even know his own intentions on the first few dates! So, the less information you give when you're declining his sexual hospitality, the better.

Don't Use a Token "No"

....

One other by-product of the sexual double standard is the common use of the "token no." In an effort not to appear sexually "easy," women will often say no to sex while retaining warm energy and physical closeness. Their "no" is murmured while they're kissing a man or lying in his arms. This is very confusing for guys. Your mouth says one thing, but your body says another. This is a mixed message for sure, and more than a few date rape cases have been tried based on that giant misunderstanding.

Dr. Metts, whose work at Illinois State University focuses on sexual communication, says the "token no" can be a dangerous strategy. "My advice to young women who want to be polite to a potential partner is to say 'No' very directly and then to move away from the intimate context. Literally stand up, move across the room, or ask to be taken home. It is a misperception that a man's feelings will be hurt or that he will feel discounted if his date refuses to have sex. No explanation is necessary, but if one is given, it must be clear. To simply say 'I am not ready yet' can be interpreted as 'I will be ready for sex in about five minutes.' A better statement is 'I do not want to have sex. I am not being coy and am not playing a game. I do not want to have sex.'"

Sadly, so many men have obtained sex after a "token no" that many of them regard it as part of foreplay. Know that in *The 30-Day Love Detox*, words aren't enough. You must also say it with action.

Like a Postmodern Virgin

I interviewed a huge range of women for this book—either via e-mail, phone, or in person. I cast a wide net by simply stating I wanted to talk to single women ages 21 to 38 and married women and mothers about how they came to be in a committed relationship. I was surprised to find that some of the married women I interviewed had been virgins until their wedding nights. Really! In this day and age. And they weren't home-schooled religious zealots who had checked out of popular culture. One was a Harvard graduate. Another was an investment banker on Wall Street. A third is now a university professor in France. And they were all feminists. Granted, most had a religious teaching that formed the basis for their decision. But the Add Health study on virginal college students showed that fear of pregnancy or an STD or that their education would get waylaid ranked way above religion as the reason most modern virgins abstain from sex.[18]

One such woman is Sarah Hinlicky Wilson, assistant research professor at the Institute for Ecumenical Research in Strasbourg, France. She's now 36, married, and the mother of one son. As a single woman at the tender age of 22, she wrote an explosive blog called Subversive Virginity that still gets its share of online traffic from curiosity seekers and postmodern virgins looking for inspiration. Her feminist take on virginity is notable because her thoughts underscore the power a woman attains when she removes her vagina from the high-supply sexual economy:

> The pretense that aggression and power-mongering are the only options for female sexual success has opened the door to predatory men. The imbalance of power becomes greater than ever in a culture of easy access. Against this system of mutual exploitation stands the more compelling alternative of virginity. It escapes the ruthless cycle of winning and losing because it refuses to play the game. The promiscuous

of both sexes will take their cheap shots at one another, disguising infidelity and self-ishness as freedom and independence, and blaming the aftermath on one another. But no one can claim control over a virgin. Vir-ginity is not a matter of asserting power in order to manipulate. It is a refusal to exploit or be exploited. That is real, and responsible, power.[19]

I don't know about you, but I got a chill when I read that because she's certainly right about one thing: Choos-ing not to have sex with a man isn't caving to a patriarchal notion that "good" women should remain chaste. Plenty of good women have lots of great sex with loving men who deserve it. Choosing not to have sex with a man is taking control. It's taking back the power. Patriarchy brought us this high-supply sexual culture. Trust me. Women didn't invent hookups.

I'm not suggesting we all suddenly incarnate ourselves into reclaimed virgins, but there are some lessons we can take from the example of these strong women. And I do think there's value in reassessing our behaviors and our definition of freedom.

Virgins can teach us something about the art of "No" because they have some serious skills when it comes to declining sex. I was fascinated to learn how women had been able to remain virgins for years, living in such a sexu-alized culture and dating in a high-supply sexual economy. When I interviewed each one, I inquired about how they said "No," hoping for tips and strategies, but instead, I heard the same resounding theme over and over. That is, when you're truly clear with yourself—when you have a deep resolve—then saying "No" comes easily and naturally.

When to Say Yes to Sex

1. After you've been in regular, consistent contact for at least 30 days (the longer the better). That contact should include mostly face and phone time and less text and e-mail.

2. After he has expressed some feelings of love. He may not blatantly say "I love you," but he may say something like, "I like you a lot" or "Maybe you can be my girl." This shows that he understands that feelings and sex go together.

3. You and he have had a conversation about monogamy and what the clear rules will be in this sexual relationship. Will he be exclusive to you? Ask him!

On the other hand, trying to decline sex when we're feeling ambivalent is a path to failure. Women roll over easily when we don't have deep conviction.

"When we are solid inside ourselves, we also get less resistance from men," said a 33-year-old senior vice president at a Wall Street investment firm who remained a virgin until her wedding night at age 29. "It was really easy to say no because I was so resolute. I didn't get a lot of pressure."

The odd time she did get pressure, her response was something any man with values couldn't argue with: "I am waiting until marriage. It's been incredibly difficult, but it's something I want to give my future husband: a sex life free of STDs, emotional baggage, and memories of others."

A Harvard business school graduate strutted her self-esteem when she told me she loved when modern men—accustomed to a junk food sexual diet—used that age-old pressure "If I don't get it from you, I'm going to get it from someone else." Player men know that women's fear of abandonment will help them score. Still a virgin at 25, this attractive young woman giggled as she told me her favorite response is to smile and respond with "Actually, you can't get sex with me from someone else."

The Big Payoff

Let's not forget the purpose of this dating and sex diet. Giving a man time and space to send you signals about his intentions is a gift to a commitment-oriented guy. Good guys really want to wait (although they'll take sex if it's available) because they're looking to commit to you for the long haul. Delaying sex helps you gain power to make wise cavewoman choices that will directly affect your future as a mate and mother. And it will help you build that magical relationship glue called *emotional intimacy*.

"When the onset of a sexual relationship is delayed, it helps couples determine more thoroughly their ability to develop emotional, intellectual, and relational intimacy," says Dr. Busby. "Early sexual involvement is so overwhelming physiologically and even emotionally that it can cloud the ability to see clearly in these other areas."

The 30-Day Love Detox will help you build solid relationship skills you can use down the line, not just for the short term. Sure, you want to be fun, hot, flexible, and attractive—but you also need to be honest, empathetic, firm, and unafraid of conflict. When you're having sex, you aren't developing the skills you'll need for a long-term relationship. Bottom line: Waiting to have sex prevents a whole lot of heartbreak and increases your chances for a long-term commitment.

Man Withdrawal Syndrome

"If I'm not getting enough attention from guys, I go out and try to get more. If I don't have a lot of guy attention, it affects how I perceive myself. I know it's bad."

The most promising message in this statement by a 22-year-old psychology student is that she's aware of her insecurities and how bound her self-esteem is to reactions from men. Other women aren't so lucky. They tap on keyboards and smartphones scanning for digital compliments. They use finely tuned girl radar in the real world to search for guys who might be checking them out. They may target one man but rarely give up communication with a few backup choices and past lovers who stroke their female egos.

Women may have reached a historic zenith of power in

their careers, but at no time in history have women felt so powerless in terms of relationships. The backward sexual economy has men calling the shots sexually and women surrendering to a male definition of love—meaning, they accept less commitment and place more emphasis on their looks for self-esteem.

"Even when I am in a relationship, I always keep a couple guy friends on the side who I text and talk to, even about my relationship," said a 25-year-old pharmaceutical sales representative, a classic example of a male attention junkie. Who knows if these men exist to keep her boyfriend on his toes or as a backup plan, but either way, it's a betrayal of sorts that prevents her from maintaining a lasting, fulfilling relationship.

This is the antithesis of having a healthy, emotionally intimate attachment. It even borders on boundary violations. A "guy friend" probably shouldn't be privy to information about your romantic relationship. Think about it. Is your platonic male friend really going to help you succeed with his competition? And how does your significant other feel about you sharing intimate details with other dudes?

If you haven't seen the movie *When Harry Met Sally*, allow me to explain. All heterosexual single men who have private access to your thoughts and feelings are likely waiting in the wings. No matter how hard you've worked to erect clear boundaries and establish you're not interested in a sexual relationship, I promise you, a tiny part of him still has hopes. This very thing happened to a friend of mine recently. She had a stalwart guy friend through a long, painful marriage and a couple years of unhappy single life. But the minute she fell deeply in love with someone else, her friend became negative, angry, and even a little depressed. My bet? He still had fantasies of being her boyfriend.

The Five Men in Your Comfort Zone

Most single women today aren't content with the attention of one man. Relationships today are just too undefined and too fragile. Instead, women tend to keep a cadre of loose attachments with about five men who help them deal with the anxiety of being single.

We all have a first love—that high school or college sweetheart who stole our heart behind the football bleachers. As time goes by, you've forgotten many of the reasons why you broke up with him and begin to harbor a quiet fantasy that if all else fails, you could maybe resurrect that relationship. So, you give him a call over the holidays and sometimes drop him a birthday card. It's a way to stay a little in touch. Just in case.

There's also a more recent ex-boyfriend. This was the guy you thought was "the one," but the timing wasn't right or the flame burned out when you moved in together. But otherwise, it was a good relationship. Right? I mean, if it was *all bad*, why is he still e-mailing occasionally? He gives great advice on business decisions, and you're comforted that he's one of the few guys who truly understand you. You have history together. Maybe it could work out in the future.

Then, there's Mr. Right Now. He's the most tenuous of all because we haven't actually bagged him yet as a boyfriend. Oh, you may be sleeping together. And your heart skips a beat when you see his texts, but this is far from a committed relationship. It's the one that gives you the most anxiety. (Note: When your stomach flip-flops over the fragility of a relationship, that shouldn't be confused with actual feelings of love.)

That's why you have Mr. Facebook Friend. He represents a possible future opportunity. You may know him in the real world or through one of your friends. He loves to flirt online, so you know he likes you. And his private messages make you feel really good. He could be a good backup plan if Mr. Right Now becomes Mr. Yesterday.

In the meantime, there's that guy in the office elevator. All you know about him is that he works at the law firm on the ninth floor. He carries a copy of *The New Yorker* and a venti Starbucks cup most mornings. And he always has a clever and funny comment about your platform shoes. You don't see a wedding band on him, so this means he's fair game when you need to move him a little higher up your male attention bandwidth.

I want to add here that five seems to be the minimum number of men that women juggle solely for their personal security. Plenty of women I spoke to actually have two or three Mr. Right Nows and a dozen Mr. Facebook Friends and Mr. Elevators.

Now, think about this. Would you be happy if your boyfriend, fiancé, or husband had a harem of real and virtual women? Okay, so even if you believe that most men in your world *already do*, do you really think this is the MO of the guy who's going to make a commitment to you?

Managing the attention of a cluster of men is a poor substitute for real internal power and committed love. I advise you to detox all the false attention. Unless a guy is willing to pick up the phone, meet you regularly in the real world, and have conversations that involve the real "F" word (feelings), then he's a junk food man giving you poor emotional nutrition. He might taste good in small bites, but a life filled with junk food men who supply endless sexual attention is a woman's version of porn. And it can play havoc with your ability to be a committed mate.

Your Hottest Body Part

....

I asked my 8-year-old daughter, "What's your most attractive and powerful body part?"

"My stomach," she offered. I wasn't sure if she meant her budding six-pack or the fact that ice cream feels so powerful going in there, but I pressed forward.

"Nope," I said. "Guess again."

The little angel looked completely befuddled, but she took a giant leap and in a soft, questioning voice ventured with what appeared to be an outlier in her mind's eye. "My brain?"

I exhaled. Then, I did the touchdown cheer. And this is the message I have for you. Commitment-minded men—and there are plenty—are looking for commitment-minded women with high self-esteem. Confidence is sexy when it comes bottled by any gender. But so many women lose confidence when male attention wanes.

Sociology professor Mark Regnerus, PhD, explains why women think they need male attention for power. They think the attention itself makes them attractive rather than some internal feeling of self-worth.[1] "Not a few women, ignorant or disbelieving of basic sexual economics, imagine that power is found in generating male desire," he wrote in an e-mail to me. "On the contrary, most any woman with a pulse can generate some male desire."

Ouch! Are you saying all those flirtatious e-mails, Facebook messages, and Twitter tweets don't make us desirable? You mean just about any woman can generate them?

In a word, yes. All that digital static from men is just pretend power. Real power lies in loving yourself enough to go against your culture. What makes us desirable is our ability to maintain clear personal boundaries independent of male desire. And real feminine power is emotional power, not sexual power. The wide bandwidth of male attention that so many women are addicted to is just sexual power. And that's only a tiny ingredient in having a great relationship.

Stage One Withdrawal

If you've been mainlining male attention for the last few years, you'll notice a few things that will happen once you begin to practice the love detox in earnest. First of all, in the beginning, most men will become intrigued and pursue you harder.

Anita is an attorney in Alabama. She represents the group of women who have the highest rate of marriage in the country: educated women with conservative political views who live in the South. Her culture has taught her to practice a version of the love detox—that is, waiting months before engaging in sex with a man—and this, she tells me, makes men fall in serious love with her. While she's busy determining their fitness as a long-term mate, they're busy falling head over heels. She finds this hysterical. This doesn't mean they're all commitment-oriented men. It means they've been injected with a love drug.

You've heard about oysters and caviar. How about champagne and a warm bath? Trust me, none of these have been proven as a true aphrodisiac (a substance that supposedly increases sexual desire; the name comes from Aphrodite, the Greek goddess of sensuality and love).

Throughout history, many foods and drinks have had a reputation for making sex more attainable and/or pleasurable. However, from a historical and scientific standpoint, the alleged results are mainly due to a belief by their users that they are effective. Yep, a placebo effect. But there's one thing that works most of the time, and it's the very thing you're going to be handing out during *The 30-Day Love Detox*.

It's the word *no*. Spoken loudly or quietly—spoken in behavior or lack of behavior—the word *no* makes a sexual suitor sit up and take notice. It's human nature to want what you can't have, but psychologists have a mathematical formula when it comes to sex.

AROUSAL + OBSTACLE = EROTIC SEX

A psychological obstacle makes physical arousal more intense. San Francisco–based psychotherapist Jack Moran, PhD, described it well in his book *The Erotic Mind*. He explains that partners need some sort of resistance to heighten arousal and motivate sexual pursuit.[2] It's one of the reasons women become so aroused by bad boys. Their emotional unavailability is the psychological obstacle.

Now think back to your most exciting sexual encounter. Was it intergenerational? Interracial? Would your parents have hated him? Was he a bad boy? Was he unavailable in some way? Maybe a married boss? Nothing like an obstacle—be it a cultural or personal taboo—to get our juices flowing.

But having a healthy long-term committed relationship is your goal here. Not some sexual high. I'm guessing you've already had a few of those. In the beginning of the love detox, you need to keep your mind on the mission. Don't get distracted by the short-term increase in male attention. And don't interpret this increase in pursuit as evidence that he has long-term potential. Only time will tell. You're looking for him to sacrifice in some modern way, not just increase interest and pressure.

Stage Two Withdrawal

If you keep following the prescription for the love detox—no wet kisses, no groping, no sexts, no flirty e-mails—and you keep it up for 30 days (or longer!), you'll notice something beginning to happen. Slowly, almost without your noticing, that bandwidth of male attention will begin to shrink. You'll log into Facebook and see fewer messages. Texts from players and commitment phobes who used to chirp out daily on your smartphone will disappear for days at a time. And then weeks. And then, they'll drop off completely. Ladies, this won't feel good.

You might feel lonely and abandoned and find yourself "just browsing" online dating sites. You might find yourself with an urge to go stir up some male attention, but I advise against this. Things will slow down. Your life will become quieter. You'll feel the full impact of the backward sexual economy. Most men will move on to women who'll give them easy sex.

But you don't need most men. You don't need them for your self-esteem. You don't need them for financial support. You don't need them for sexual pleasure. (If you disagree with this, go back and read the sexual myths from Chapter 6.) You don't need most men for your self-worth or even for your happiness. You just need *one* man for a healthy relationship.

Nonetheless, as you enter stage two of the love detox, you'll find yourself second-guessing my advice. You'll flirt with the idea that maybe the old way was better. I mean, at least when you had many short-term relationships, you felt you had some kind of choice. But where's the choice when there seems to be no one to choose from?

This is when I'll ask you to take a deep breath. This is the time to engage your cavewoman wisdom. This is the time to light a candle, meditate, and begin to believe in *yourself.* You can do this. You can make a good choice this time. And you'll do it by giving yourself and the men you meet the gift of time. Create some space for him to display his intentions. You owe him that. He's a good guy.

While you detox, try the following coping strategies. These tips will help you stay sane when your culture barks messages that run counterintuitive to your natural biology.

Managing Man Withdrawal Syndrome

1. Accept that your discomfort is real and that other people may not understand it. You may experience separation anxiety and heightened abandonment issues. These are real symptoms with real biological consequences. You may experience absentmindedness, sleeplessness, and eating changes. (You might eat too much or too little.) You might find yourself feeling angry and on edge. Or you may find yourself tearing up at couples walking in the park hand in hand. Know that all of this is normal.

2. Use the logical side of your brain to reassure yourself that the man gap created by the love detox is temporary. Within a few months, as you change your habits, new and different men will show up in your radar. Studies on grieving and depression show that those people with an optimistic outlook on the future heal faster.[3] Hope is paramount to the love detox.

3. Calm yourself with the mantra that your feelings are a necessary part of your healing. After an addict (one who's addicted to food, alcohol, or drugs) completes the physical withdrawal stage, a host of surprising and terrifying feelings bubble to the surface. These are the very feelings they suppressed with their self-medication. Getting off an addiction to short-term relationships can also feel scary and might even bring up some painful childhood memories.

4. See a therapist. Your love detox will be easier with a partner to help you through things. There are many affordable clinics and counseling centers. See "Finding an Affordable Therapist."

5. Make a plan for vulnerable times. Have a list of people you can e-mail, text, call, or chat with in order to find connection. Not comfort men and junk food men! Stick with people you've had positive relationships with, such as parents, siblings, your children, or close girlfriends. Use these positive relationships as a way to bolster your self-esteem when you might be feeling lonely or depressed.

Finding an Affordable Therapist

Check your health insurance. Many insurance carriers cover mental health services (although there may be a cap on how many sessions they'll cover) and may even provide a list of affordable "in-network" therapists in your area.

Try university counseling centers. If your local university offers a psychology program, there's a good chance they offer a sliding-scale fee structure—a price based on the ability to pay.

Look into professional training centers. Most large cities have psychology graduate schools that run counseling centers staffed by PhD students. All these students are supervised by practicing therapists. Google the words "psychotherapy institute" along with your city name.

Call and ask. Plenty of therapists in private practice do a few hours a week of pro bono work or therapy with clients who can afford to pay only a small fee. It doesn't hurt to call and ask.

6. Replace male attention with other kinds of attention. Do charity work that puts you face-to-face with the people you're helping. Schedule a regular girls night in to watch a movie (not a night out at a bar watching your girlfriends snort male attention).

7. Treat yourself well. These are stressful times. You're changing your energy signals and ultimately inviting in a new kind of man. This can be downright uncomfortable. But while you're changing your world, make sure you eat right, drink less, and exercise more.

8. Replace sexual touch with human touch. If you can afford it, get a weekly massage so your body gets the touch it's accustomed to. If you have a pet, cuddle up. Take your sister's kids to the park for a rowdy game of "tackle the aunt." Visit a nursing home and hold the hand of a touch-deprived elderly person. If your mom lives near, give her a giant hug. Recognize that some of the emotional withdrawal you're feeling is related to a physical reaction to the loss of touch. And yes, if you are so inclined, by all means use this time to learn how to play your own sexual instrument and learn what really turns you on. Beware of vibrators, however. Plenty of women actually get addicted to mechanical stimulation and have trouble reaching climax when intimate with a partner. Stay as natural as possible.

Renew Your Faith in Men

While you're waiting, you might want to re-evaluate your perceptions of men. I can't tell you how many women in my focus groups regressed to male bashing when I asked them to tell me relationship stories. No doubt about it. There are troops of angry single women out there. They feel the deck is stacked against them and haven't found a way to win the game. So they blame men.

Some of you may even have found yourselves feeling angry while reading some of the social science in this book. I won't lie to you. I have had more than a few college women walk out of my lecture halls when I start talking about female sexual restraint. It feels old-fashioned and patriarchal. The comments on some of my blogs from women who have been fed a false bill of goods about fertility and female sexuality reflect a misunderstanding that somehow I'm not supportive of female sexual freedom. Nothing could be further from the truth. I'm all for sexual freedom, even if it includes swinging from a chandelier in a French maid's uniform with your husband while your three kids are asleep upstairs! More than anything, I endorse the freedom to be a mother and the freedom to have the best outcomes for your children. Given the current limitations in cultural support for single mothers, I also hope you send signals that invite in a man who can be an involved father. And for that, you need less sex in the short term.

And I have faith in men. Believe it or not, men aren't so happy with this high-supply sexual economy either. Back in my *Sex and the City* days, I had more than a couple men actually look at me with disappointment the morning after. "I wanted to court you," sighed one music industry executive. Another date, a film director, got angry with me because he felt I had "played" him.

Most men want love and commitment, too; they just aren't as motivated as women to change things. Men have no fertility window; they're less susceptible to STDs; they're more vulnerable to loss of assets after divorce; and they're pressured to have lots of sex. So they're not encouraged to control themselves. Many men count on women to be the custodians of the social order.

Just as you're pressured to conform to an acceptable ideal of modern female sexual behavior that says you should be having lots of sex but not too much, men are also trapped in a narrow band. That is, our culture expects men to always want sex with as many partners as possible. This simply isn't true. In fact, some men are relieved when women decline sex. They're happy to wait for sex.

In a recent study of 4,300 men in Australia, 12 percent of men between ages 16 and 24 said they wanted less sex.[4] And this was the highest proportion of any age group. I know this is a small minority, but remember, men generally lie "up" rather than "down" when it comes to sex surveys, bragging about the number of partners and sexual frequency to satisfy the narrative pressured by a masculine culture. And it's notable that the group most often considered to have insatiable sexual appetites—young men—had the largest proportion of desire for less sex.

"I think it was always a bit of a myth that *all* men are gagging for it all the time," the study's lead researcher, Juliet Richters, PhD, associate professor in sexual health at the University of New South Wales, wrote in an e-mail to me. "The main pressure for men to have sex comes from other men—always teasing, showing off, running the losers down."

The truth is, most men are accustomed to waiting for sex. The National Longitudinal Study of Adolescent Health data offers other glimpses into how men behave sexually. For example, 64 percent of young men already wait nearly two weeks for sex with a new dating partner. Forty-nine percent of men have sex within thirty days, but that means that *more than half the men you may meet* are quite accustomed to waiting at least a month for sex.[5] Granted, 30 percent of young men have sexual relationships that don't involve love or romance at all, but these are the 30 percent who'll move away fast when you do *The 30-Day*

Love Detox. Don't worry. You haven't lost much. These guys aren't likely to marry, and if they do, they'll have trouble being faithful.

Making Yourself Marketable

....

The 30-Day Love Detox isn't a prescription to sit at home licking your wounds and eating ice cream. It's a prescription to take charge of your love life. And you start by understanding what commitment-oriented men look for in a long-term partner.

David Buss, PhD, evolutionary psychologist and coauthor of *Why Women Have Sex: Understanding Sexual Motivations from Adventure to Revenge (and Everything in Between)*, says the only way to compete successfully for desirable men is by embodying what men want.[6] "If women are seeking a long-term mate, they need to embody what men want in a long-term mate. Although attractiveness is important, other qualities include loyalty, fidelity, kindness, intelligence, dependability, and good health. These are all qualities that are under women's control—at least to some degree."

Men want honesty, fidelity, and kindness. Sounds very familiar—the very traits you should be looking for in a man. So, I ask, with all due respect, how can we seek that which we can't be? *The 30-Day Love Detox* is an opportunity to become the very partner you desire.

It's also an opportunity to migrate to a more supportive social circle. If your friends prefer to focus on short-term relationships, then you might need to leave the party. First, you don't need to be many degrees of separation to get a bad reputation. (Remember, while we don't believe in double standards, research shows that most men still do.[7]) Second, your social circle is like honey to bees. Don't get stung by the players they attract. Good men stay out of the hive.

Instead, as boring as it may seem, your best odds of success will come when you start to hang out with happy couples. Sixty percent of married couples meet through a married friend.[8] Marriage is like a born-again religion. Once couples have marital bliss, they're compelled to share it. I must warn you, though: It will take some time and you may feel like the third or fifth wheel at a few dinner tables, but before long, one of those married women will find a dude at her office for you. (One thing's for sure, married women don't like to keep a single girlfriend around their husbands for too long!)

And if you live in a female-dominant world, and have the educational or career flexibility, you might decide to work or study in a city where there are more single men than women (see the chart). Like the love detox itself, moving to a more female-friendly locale increases your statistical probability of having a long-term relationship. Certain pockets of American culture are very supportive of

Cities with More Single Men Than Women

1. Los Angeles
2. San Francisco
3. Seattle
4. Denver
5. Dallas

old-fashioned relationships, so if your eggs are getting old and you want marriage, you might want to get your Spinning-class butt to a red state, rent a condo near a military base, and sit in the back pew of a church. I'm joking, of course, but only sort of. As we talked about in Chapter 4, you know how much time you have and what kind of relationship you want. Now you need to ask yourself how you can be proactive and use your power to put your plan in action. If I were looking for a job, I'd go where the jobs are. If I were looking for a man, I'd go where more men are.

Falling Off the Detox Wagon

It's inevitable. At some point in the love detox, you'll find your willpower breaking down. You might misjudge a guy and have sex with him too soon, or you might simply say "What the hell!" and hook up one night. This is to be expected. Going cold turkey on anything is a tough walk. The key is to get back on that wagon and remind yourself about your goal. Again, if short-term relationships are fine

Cities with More Single Women Than Men

1. New York
2. Chicago
3. Miami
4. Philadelphia
5. Boston

with you, then proceed onward. But if you've made a relationship life plan, don't give up on it. Don't give up on yourself. Even the most dedicated dieter has a binge weekend. And that binge can serve as another wake-up call.

Falling off the love detox wagon might remind you about the empty feelings that sex without love can bring up. We're women, and no matter what mythology you've been served, our sexuality is different from a man's. Yes, some women can have sex without emotional connection, and I'd venture to say that group is growing, but plenty of other women haven't moved from their age-old biological urge to bond through sex. One study on one-night stands found that the majority of men in the study felt higher self-confidence and a sense of well-being after a booty call, but half the women reported negative feelings afterward and lower self-worth.[9]

So, if you fall off the wagon, I encourage you to climb back on it. Remind yourself that destructive short-term relationships have a statistical probability of failing and increase the chances that you'll miss the opportunity for real love and motherhood.

The Birth of a Mother

If your goal is to become a mother in a healthy family, know this: A healthy family blooms from two sources of health—mental and physical—and mothers are the guiding light for their entire family's health. Physically, it's wise to prepare for parenthood by avoiding STDs and unwanted pregnancies that can impact your future fertility.

But raising children also involves necessary emotional health. Sandra Metts, PhD, who researches and teaches emotional communication at the University of Illinois, says every relationship we have affects our emotional health. "Low self-esteem arising from destructive dating experiences can make a woman less resilient when facing the challenges of marriage and raising children and less likely to find useful options for dealing with family challenges. Avoid potentially problematic relationships, such as booty-call relationships, and/or make absolutely certain that you understand clearly what your partner's intentions are. It may be awkward to have the 'What are we?' conversation, but in the long term, it will prevent hurt, embarrassment, and lingering negative feelings about relationship trust and stability."

The love detox can help you become a better person *and* a better future mother. The growing pains associated with gaining the skills of self-control and emotional communication are short term. But the long-term benefits of mastering these skills will serve you, your children, and the generations who come after you. I encourage you to be brave and avoid fear-based decisions.

"The perceived risk in waiting too long—that he'll leave—shows just how much power men have in the modern mating market," says Dr. Regnerus. "It's time to take back some of that power, women. And you know exactly how to do that."

PART III

THE ART OF
ATTACHMENT

CHAPTER 8

He Waited! Now What?

66 **I**f anyone was going to find dysfunction attractive, it would be me," a 30-something VP at an investment firm revealed to me as she sat on my couch, nursing her third child. "When I finally found a healthy relationship, I had to go gradually. He was so proactive and sincere. This was extremely uncomfortable to me. But he didn't seem to mind my slow pace. He was secure enough not to pressure me."

Up until now, this book has taken a crystal-clear view of your relationship landscape. It has prompted you to evaluate your choices and make a clear plan for your relationship life. And it's given you a hard-core prescription for how to increase your odds of getting what you want. Now it's time for you to learn some relationship-building skills.

I know you need these and I'll tell you how I know. The more I interviewed and corresponded by e-mail with researchers in human attachment, the more I heard about increasing emotional avoidance due to "mobility." At first, I was so distracted by the sad news that nearly half the population is terrified of feelings and lean toward stormy or empty relationships that I missed the suggested cause. But the third time I heard "mobility" mentioned, I decided to investigate.

What social scientists call mobility is the new lifestyle of many Americans. It's a by-product of capitalism. Indeed, it's the way of life that many of us grew up with. We lived in lots of different neighborhoods, cities, states, and even countries as our parents sought better work or new relationships after divorce. And as we moved to new places, we became more culturally open. We got used to meeting new people, and we became flexible. That's the good part about mobility. But the ominous thing about mobility that affects our relationships is that we also learned to break up. We learned not to hold on too tight. We learned that conflict can be avoided simply by our disappearing. This is the legacy left to our generation. We learned to detach.[1]

This is exactly the opposite skill set that one needs to form a close bond—to endure the bumps of conflict and raise children who can grow up to create solid relationships themselves. *The 30-Day Love Detox*'s prescription for slow love protects you from predatory men and kind, clueless men who hit below the belt. It also bestows you with an amazing opportunity to learn, along with a partner, how to negotiate the prickly path toward a secure attachment. Many of us weren't taught the skills of emotional intimacy because, frankly, our parents didn't have the skills themselves. And I'll warn you that emotional intimacy can be scary. But it's possible to learn it at any stage of life. In this chapter, I break it down into eight simple concepts and skills that will help you grow love and trust with the man you've chosen to invite into your heart.

Becoming Attached: How to Grow Trust

....

1. LEARN COMPASSION

Compassion is kind of like empathy—the ability to sense the feelings of another—except it has one crucial distinction: Compassion includes action. It's the act of doing something positive in response to someone else's feelings.

I will be so bold as to declare that compassion is the very essence of love. Compassion is the trait we showcase when we're attracting a partner and falling in love. Compassion is the magic dust we sprinkle on our fights to help us repair the damage. And compassion is the glue that keeps couples together when the going gets boring and the grass next door looks neon.

However, the capacity to have compassion is a little tricky to acquire if you weren't parented with compassion yourself—if your parents projected their own desires on you instead of respecting you as a unique person. The good news is that the human mind is plenty malleable. Environmental conditions and intellectual processing can change how we think and feel. The first step to becoming a compassionate person is to make a commitment to practice empathy. This is the day to get out of your own head and move into the heads of others—because in case you didn't know, each and every one of us has our own unique version of reality. Yep, in every family, there are as many movies playing as there are brains perceiving.

The second step toward becoming a compassionate person (and strengthening your relationships) is to erase any negative feelings you might have about giving to another. Yes, believe it or not, some people think being supportive and kind is a sign of weakness or that putting someone else's needs ahead of their own is giving up some precious control. If this kind of belief system was programmed into your tender mind way back when, I give you permission today to let go of those notions. Instead, reprogram your brain with the idea that the "giver" is the power player in life. The receiver isn't a "taker" but is a worthy human being.

While you're waiting for your mate to come along, there are three kinds of people you can practice compassion with: strangers, acquaintances, and intimate family. With strangers and acquaintances, the practice is quite simple: Increase your eye contact. Study their faces. What's really going on with the teenager working at the drive-thru window? The teacher who sighs as she trudges into your child's class? The bank teller who carefully counts out your money? With each everyday encounter, ask yourself what kind thing—be it word or deed—you can do to improve someone else's mood.

Then, sit back and watch the magic happen. Compliments turn stone-faced strangers into beaming friends. And your friendships will improve when you put empathy into action and offer a ride, a babysitter, or some arms to help lug stuff. And don't assume you know exactly what people need. Inquire first. Then, offer goodness with no strings attached. That's true compassion. And it can be done in the smallest of ways. I sometimes stack the dishes for a waitress at a busy family restaurant to make her load easier. I open doors for strangers. I say an earnest "good morning" to people at Starbucks. I always inquire and offer help to mothers with babies and toddlers in public. These small acts of connecting teach your brain to have compassion.

Our intimate family members require a bit more gentle detective work. We need to go deeper to create emotional intimacy. There's a technique that psychotherapists often use called *reflective listening*. Reflective listening involves translating the speaker's words into your own words and feeding them back with a voice of inquiry. So, your boyfriend comes home and says, "This was such a f—ed up day." A straight inquiry might be simply, "What happened?" But with the addition of reflective listening, you might say, "Things didn't go so well for you today, and you look like you're feeling mad." Then, pause. Wait and watch. You might even reach out and touch him. A hand on the shoulder or a stroke of the hair signals to your partner that you're connected with him or her and available for support. Then let him lead the conversation, and with each moment of interjection, reflect back to his feelings so he begins to feel truly heard and supported. You might be surprised by what you hear and what you learn about the person you thought you knew so well.

Compassion is one of the skills that make relationships stronger because when we truly see and empathize with others, we become loyal to them. We tune into the same familiar news anchor and our favorite sports stars in the same way. Familiarity breeds loyalty. Compassion works on us, too. Compassion is the feeling we can use to love ourselves more. To accept our own flawed path and ill-timed lessons of life. When we can feel compassion for ourselves—that is, understand our own sufferings and do something to heal them—then we have so much more to give in a love relationship.

The next time you find yourself at an impasse with love, stop and entertain the feeling of compassion. Are you being too hard on yourself? Are you being too hard on that other human being in your life? Dig deep at these moments to scoop from the river of compassion that flows inside every person. Compassion is the one thing that works every time to build trust and emotional intimacy.

2. FOSTER INTERDEPENDENCE

We're raised to be independent. Our mothers were pushed to move us quickly from womb to dorm room. And we're praised for every task accomplished without assistance. This is modern American capitalism's way of creating a flexible, mobile workforce. At the same time, we're told that being "needy" is a sign of weakness and to beware of smothering boyfriends. But nowhere have we been taught about healthy interdependence.

Because that's what a long-term relationship is. It's a mutual exchange of care. And care can't be fairly exchanged unless we have the skills to communicate our needs and to comfortably receive care. Sadly, when this generation of super-achieving women finds themselves in the very needy place of first-time motherhood, having to ask for care feels like such a failure. So they bark out commands to the men who used to read their texts—now fully expecting them to read their minds. I've seen this too many times. A woman's necessary neediness feels like a weakness, and this causes her to boil with anger because she "has to ask." This prompts a vicious cycle of anger because seldom do our needs get met when we're summoning care with dragon breath.

Healthy relationships are neither too independent (partners don't lean on each other much) nor codependent (no one can remember whose problem is whose). A good relationship is something in between. To have intimacy, one must be able to not only give care but also learn to receive care comfortably.

3. COMMUNICATE EMOTIONS

Having emotional language skills is crucial to not only the relationships we have with others but also the relationship we have with ourselves. If we can't name our feelings and share them, we're a long way off from being able to process them and use them in a healthy way. Having an honest emotional vocabulary is crucial to emotional intimacy, although this communication art is easier for some of us than others.

Men and boys are socialized to express less emotional communication, and I think they're also biologically wired to have less emotional awareness than women. Research confirms that men actually feel less guilt than women.[2] There's even a diagnosis in the therapist's bible of mental disorders—the *DSM*—called alexithymia, which basically means an inability to connect feelings with words. In recent years, a Harvard professor, Ron Levant, EdD, came up with the phrase *normative male alexithymia* to describe how American males are culturally conditioned to repress their vulnerable and caring emotions, causing them to become underdeveloped in emotional expressiveness.[3]

But a fear of talking about feelings is an equal opportunity affliction. Because feminism gave way to the no-rules relationship revolution—an age where emotions are less and less risked—many women have followed the example of men. I'd venture to say that women's greatest assets—an awareness of emotions and verbal skills—have been abandoned by too many of our gender.

The solution? To delve into the sea of honest communication that focuses on personal feelings rather than points fingers at others. One of the reasons this is a challenge for some is that this important skill was neither taught nor modeled by our parents. Parents of the 1960s and 1970s more often practiced critical parenting rather than emotionally intimate parenting. Critical parenting sounds like this: "Brittany, you're a messy girl! Look at that disgusting room. No TV for you, bad girl!" Emotionally intimate parenting sounds like this: "Brittany, I feel angry when I have to clean up your mess, and I want you to feel proud of yourself. So, I'm going to help you become neater by rewarding you with TV after you clean your room." See the focus on feelings? In this case, the feelings of anger and pride are expressed with a positive reward instead of using shame as the behavior shaper.

Assuming you were parented in the more common, critical way, here's a crash course in how to use emotional language to grow intimacy in all your relationships. First of all, in every communication, try to identify your own feelings and express them as a reaction to someone's behavior rather than an assault on their behavior. People get less defensive when they hear the words "I feel" than when they hear "You are."

Remember to use emotional words when you set a boundary or offer a criticism. We talked about them earlier: I feel nervous, happy, sad, angry, disappointed, hopeful, ignored, embarrassed, envious, jealous, lonely, excited, surprised, proud, scared, guilty, aroused, uncomfortable, rejected, or loved. Using emotional language is a bit terrifying at first, but trust me, it can enrich all your relationships. "I feel" quite confident about this.

4. TOLERATE SHAME

Shame. It's got to be one of the most unpleasant feelings in the human psyche. We do everything to avoid it. Most of our cherished psychological defenses—repression, denial, rationalization, and even humor—are designed to defend ourselves from feelings of shame. Simply put, shame is that uncomfortable mixture of guilt and embarrassment basted with a little self-loathing. It can make even the most omnipotent of us squeamish. But learning to be tolerant of your own shame is crucial to building emotional intimacy with another person.

Here's why: We're not truly lovable unless we're real. Authentic people are attractive because, believe it or not, only the most healthy—the most confident—can express shame and still love themselves. And that's hot. My favorite definition of emotional intimacy is being able to tolerate seeing the flaws in your loved ones and, just as important, still loving yourself knowing your intimates can see your flaws.

Emotional intimacy is the way couples build trust and loyalty. It's the "I'll have your back if you have mine" philosophy. But it doesn't happen spontaneously. It happens over time with small personal disclosures and toe dips into the sea of authentic soul baring. On the road to making all your relationships more secure, here are a few tips for learning to tolerate shame.

Remember that some of the things you feel shame about aren't real. Talking about them can help you relieve yourself of guilt. Everyone has a few beliefs that are distortions based on early life experiences. When you begin to talk about what flaws you perceive in yourself, you'll find that most of them were invented by a child who had critical parents. Expressing your shame can help heal these distortions.

Being shame-tolerant is different from being "shameless." You still need boundaries. The key to disclosing personal information is choosing the right target. Test people with small disclosures about vulnerabilities and then see how they protect you. Learning to tolerate shame is different from not having personal boundaries. Not every relationship you have in the world will be an intimate one filled with trust. Choose your targets carefully.

Sometimes, you have to be the first to show healthy shame in order for your partner to feel safe doing it himself. If you've done something wrong or hurt someone, talk about it. Let others who are close to you see your mental process. Let them see how you make restitution to the wronged person and let them see how you eventually forgive yourself.

Finally, if another person practices authenticity with you, never shame them! So, if a friend says "I feel bad because I hit my neighbor's car," don't respond with "You should feel bad! That was wrong." I guarantee that anyone who responds to a person admitting shame with an added layer of shame will get the door on emotional communication slammed shut. Instead, you might say something like: "That's a hard feeling to have. I'm glad you shared it with me. Want me to come with you to apologize?"

Shame tolerance is one of the most crucial skills needed to create true emotional intimacy and long-lasting love. Try it in small doses. And know that feeling some shame is a sign of a healthy psyche.

5. ACCEPT HIS FLAWS, TOO

We all know the adage "Nobody's perfect." We all have flaws. Many of them we would like to change. But a few of them are here to stay, and all we can hope is that the people who love us will accept this.

I'd venture to say that the only time a human being seems to be completely void of flaws is when he or she is caught in the snare of romantic love. The chemicals associated with sexual attraction cloud our vision, and the object of our desire—for a brief few weeks or months—is a perfect partner. But this is one of nature's tricks to get us attached. Then, as sexual attraction and romantic love give birth to the workhorse of intimacy and companionship, our partner suddenly isn't so perfect anymore. Certain flaws crop up in unmistakable focus. He snores, he watches too much sports, or he spends money in a weird way.

Learning to accept the flaws of our loved ones is an important piece in building emotional intimacy. Remember, emotional intimacy is the glue that makes relationships secure—that keeps attachments steady when the world is rocking out of control. If you're harboring secret resentments toward your partner's most personal habits, you'll unknowingly cause a leak in your ship. Because even if we think we're concealing our opinions, those pesky prejudices sneak out when we're busy talking and living and loving. The unconscious knows all. And your man will know on some deep level that you don't truly accept him. That your relationship might be threatened by, say, an outsider who breezes through life without the baggage of your husband. (He'll have other baggage, of course, but you'll be blind to it at the beginning.) And this kind of insecurity is toxic to attachments.

Funny thing about our judgments: They're often pieces of ourselves pointed outward. Psychologists call it Carl Jung's "shadow." When dark parts of our personalities are too uncomfortable to tolerate, we scan the environment and point fingers at the very thing we are.[4] If you're skeptical about this concept, start to pay attention to the sources of critical gossip. The next time you hear a wagging tongue and see a pointing finger, study the source well. You'll be surprised and enlightened.

To begin a process of learning to tolerate the flaws in your loved ones, write them down. Once the list is complete, place your name at the top of the list. Look at this list and think long and hard about what your wily brain is keeping from your awareness. Tell yourself that you love yourself—all of yourself—even the flawed parts. Then, do the same for your family.

Look at their flaws again; this time, flip the trait upside down. Turn the trait into a positive. Whether you believe the flaw belongs to your family member or to you, find a way to reframe it as a positive. This is the classic glass-half-full philosophy, and you'll need it in your long-term commitments. Look at these typical household gripes:

Flaw: Snoring boyfriend

Positive Reframe: The endearing sound of a guy who's home in bed every night, not fighting in a war or being unfaithful. And as a loving girlfriend, maybe encourage him to get tested for sleep apnea!

Flaw: Stubborn boyfriend

Positive Reframe: A man who owns the word *no* and has clear boundaries. If his behavior truly frustrates you, ask him to clearly explain his rationale and why it's so important to him.

Flaw: A husband who won't do housework

Positive Reframe: A man who works hard outside the home and brings home a steady paycheck (and always unclogs the drains).

The list can go on and on, but you get the picture. Now that I've spoken about flaw acceptance, know that there can be certain flaws that are so damaging to families that acceptance isn't an option. Substance abuse, domestic violence, depression, and abusive parenting all must be healed for the family to be healthy. But don't sweat the small stuff.

6. FIGHT FAIR

I don't think you can actually call a man your boyfriend until you've had at least one fight. In fact, a first fight is a major turning point in a relationship. At that point, couples will either work through their differences and confirm their commitment or they'll realize the differences are too great and the relationship will start to dissolve. Good conflict resolution skills are crucial to healthy long-term relationships. Research shows that conflict patterns are a great way to predict divorce.[5]

Let's face it: Conflict is part of all intimate relationships. A good fight with your spouse may even be good for your health. Research shows that members of couples whose anger is suppressed die earlier than members of couples where one or both partners express their anger and resolve the conflict.[6]

Parents get angry with kids. Wives get angry with husbands. Brothers get angry with sisters. When I hear about a couple or family that "never fights," a red flag immediately waves for me. And I'm quite assured they don't have true intimacy. When two separate people join together for common life goals, clashes are inevitable. But the presence of conflict alone isn't an indicator of a relationship's health. I prefer to focus instead on the nature of how couples and families make repair. How do couples make up after a fight? With apologies, contrition, consoling, and even laughter? Or is the aftermath of anger marked by silence, distance, and a new rule to never speak about the fight's subject?

Fair fighting means using words that identify your feelings rather than blame and point fingers. Easier said than done. Even though psychotherapists stress that we should focus on our feelings rather than level accusations, even the most educated of us resort to blaming sentences that begin with the word *You*. That alone doesn't indicate a "bad fight" unless it's also followed by vicious name calling. Name calling is a bad sign. It indicates that one partner has temporarily forgotten the other's identity and has substituted it with a skewed stereotype. It's hard to drop those evil caricatures once our minds have created them. If you see him as a loser and tell him that over and over, you're also rewiring your brain to believe this is true. One other thing to consider is the amount of voice time allotted each arguer. If the yelling is terribly lopsided and one partner gets more airtime, then something else is going on: either intimidation by the loudmouth or an emotional retreat by the other. Both things aren't fighting fair.

As injurious as a fight can be, the biggest determinant of whether it's a "good fight" is the way repair is made afterward. There are many unique ways couples come back into their relationship after a fight. Notes left by the morning coffee pot, flowers at the office, and—my favorite—off-the-charts makeup sex. But the important thing to remember is that love and respect can return.

Dangerous aftermaths include icy treatment for days on end. Little jabs thrown into unrelated conversations. Passive-aggressive retaliatory behavior. And, worst of all, a fight that morphs into other fights that get flooded with material from old injuries: "Remember the time you . . ."

The best way to learn to have "good fights" is to establish ground rules before any fighting begins. Men love rules of the game. It reminds them of sports and makes fighting a healthy challenge rather than a confusing battle with a

When "Going to Bed Mad" Is a Good Idea

Many couples have a fair fighting rule that insists they never go to sleep until they've resolved their conflict. But when you're tired, stressed, and maybe a little drunk and the hour is late, the odds that you'll resolve this conflict shrink by the minute.

My advice: Agree to revisit the argument after a good night's sleep.

scary, invisible opponent. Some ground rules might include no name-calling, no stonewalling, no fighting in front of the kids, and, most important, scheduled makeup time the next day. It's also important to understand that each person has his or her own fighting style that must be respected. A man who walks out the door for a brisk walk during an argument may not be rejecting you; he may be protecting you from a shift from words to action. Some people need a timeout to regroup and think during a fight. The time to talk about fighting styles, of course, is when you're not fighting.

Studies on couples' conflict styles show that the two most important ingredients to healthy fighting are empathy and humor. When you're feeling unheard, disrespected, or on the losing end of a power struggle, try as hard as you can to put yourself in your partner's shoes. Imagine you're on the other side of the dynamic, battling with the likes of *you*. Best of all is to find comedy in your tragedy. If you can muster the brainpower, step outside your fight and imagine you're a fly on the wall. Reframe your dialogue as a script from a *Saturday Night Live* skit or a prime-time sitcom. Now listen to how silly you sound!

The most important ingredient during a conflict is the knowledge that love can return. Spirited negotiation is all part of building intimacy. When I once commented to my favorite bickering couple that I noticed there's love behind their arguments, the husband said: "There's no love behind our arguments. It's all sport." Then, he winked. Even in conflict, there can be a bond and a secret agreement to respect each other.

7. SHOW GRATITUDE

There's no better way to enhance intimacy than to show gratitude. We all get busy. And the little things we used to do for our partners often get forgotten as we settle down into a secure attachment. But stopping to appreciate that attachment is like kryptonite to a relationship. Small acts of gratitude can really boost a relationship.[7] Think about it: When was the last time you picked up his dry cleaning? Brought a latte by his office? Planned a home-cooked dinner to celebrate something? Or simply gave him space to watch his game in peace?

Maybe you just need to express your gratitude more with words. You can strengthen your emotional bond simply by expressing words of thanks and gratitude. Daily gratefulness is how healthy relationships stay close.

8. EMBRACE RATIONAL LOVE

Couples who believe they've fallen "out of love" with each other are experiencing feelings of loss of the chemical high that goes along with romantic love, but they haven't replaced those feelings with commitment. When people make an intellectual decision to love and keep their vows to the relationship, they grow feelings of empowerment and pride of accomplishment that actually help the relationship get through tough times.

A landmark study conducted by psychologists at UCLA looked at intellectual commitment and divorce. They followed 172 married couples for eleven years, and the most startling finding was that those couples who had the ability to stay committed during times of stress were most likely to be happier and stay married.[8]

"It's easy to be committed to your relationship when it's going well," said senior study author Thomas Bradbury, PhD, a psychology professor who codirects the Relationship Institute at UCLA. "As a relationship changes, however, shouldn't you say at some point something like, 'I'm committed to this relationship, but it's not going very well—I need to have some resolve, make some sacrifices, and take the steps I need to take to keep this relationship moving forward. It's not just that I like the relationship, which is true, but that I'm going to step up and take active steps to maintain this relationship, even if it means I'm not going to get my way in certain areas'?"

Strong couples are willing to make sacrifices for the relationship. They don't tend to dig in their heels during an argument, and they're able to ask themselves "Do I need to win this battle or preserve the relationship?" This is intellectual love. The relationship itself is steered by rational choice instead of some fading romantic high.

Establish Your Relationship System

The time to begin to use all these skills of emotional intimacy is from the get-go. As soon as he begins to exhibit some clear actions and words that he's commitment oriented, you may need to lead the way toward emotional intimacy. At the very beginning of a relationship, when partners are exploring each other and slowly dropping walls, there's a need to erect some emotional boundaries. It's perfectly honest and even attractive to tell a man you don't know him well enough to disclose something yet. Too often, women hurt themselves in the early stages by assuming a man is as emotionally available as they are.

"Women are more prone to falling in love really early in a relationship and assuming that it is or should be exclusive when the man is still looking around and does not make the same assumptions about exclusivity," Juliet Richters, PhD, associate professor in sexual health at the University of New South Wales, wrote in an e-mail to me.

That's why the sequencing of emotional commitment and sexual exclusivity is so crucial to a healthy relationship. The onset of sex is the biggest turning point in a relationship. According to Sandra Metts, PhD, of the University of Illinois: "Dating relationships tend to move through a series of 'turning points' or events that either strengthen or dissolve the relationship. First, sexual involvement is one of those turning points in most dating relationships. Research indicates that when a couple has explicitly stated 'I love you' and expressed commitment to the partner before serious sexual involvement, the sexual turning point enhances both relationship satisfaction and commitment. By contrast, when a couple engages in sexual activity and then later says 'I love you' and expresses commitment, the relationship is less satisfying and less stable."

Of course, it's fair to say that plenty of modern couples who move fast toward the bedroom do express words of love as affection but only as a token way to frame the sexual act. In other words, people know that love should come before sex, so they say the words even when they aren't sure. Even this can be helpful because it indicates that the partners know the role of emotions in sex. Says Dr. Metts: "Whether a couple maintains sexual exclusivity is, of course, a matter of enduring commitment, moral standards, and emerging circumstances. However, it's more likely to be maintained if the traditional sequence of love and commitment prior to sexual involvement is followed."

All of my research and interviews with some of the best minds in human mating have helped me understand sex and its role in healthy relationships: Sex is rarely a stepping-stone to a relationship. But intimate relationships that use

How to Make a Communication Sandwich

When you need to criticize and be heard, timing is crucial. Find a quiet moment when he's not multitasking, the team isn't in the playoffs, and he's had a relatively good day so far. Next, make a communication sandwich. It's a compliment as the base, followed by a carefully worded criticism in the middle, followed by another compliment on top. The theory is that his mind will be so fortified by the goodwill you're sending that he'll be more open to the sour note in the middle. Here's an example: Your boyfriend isn't participating in enough relationship-building activities. You'd like to see him do more things with you.

Here's how the conversation might go badly (with criticism and a threat): "You never take me out anymore! If you don't put some romance back into our lives, you're going to lose me."

Here's how it can go well: "Babe, remember when you took me to the Hollywood Bowl and we had that picnic and music under the stars? Have I told you lately how much I loved that night? I'd like to have dates like that together more often. I love to be seen in public holding hands with you. It makes women so envious."

A compliment about a previous date. A clear statement about your needs. Another compliment on top. That's a great communication sandwich!

all the skills in this chapter are great stepping-stones to exciting sex. Hot sex early on in a relationship decreases your chances for long-term love. And the greater number of previous sex partners people have, the harder it is to maintain monogamy.

In her provocative book *The Defining Decade: Why Your Twenties Matter—And How to Make the Most of Them Now*, psychotherapist Meg Jay, PhD, says it's ironic that so many women are participating in short-term relationships as a way to audition mates and reduce their chances of settling for something less than perfect. Instead, they're settling for downright bad relationships.[9]

"Too many young women squander precious years by settling for no-criteria or low-criteria relationships that do little more than teach bad habits or make them feel bad about themselves," says Dr. Jay, whose practice is chock-full of confused single women. "When it does come time to commit, such as when friends start walking down the aisle on Facebook, we can feel so downtrodden or so rushed that our choices are no better—and maybe even worse—for all of our so-called practice. We realize we have been conned into spending year after year practicing all the wrong things."

I want to remind you that you have the power to change your life. It won't be easy. You're up against a culture of media and peers who bought—lock, stock, and barrel—the idea that sexual freedom is paramount to emotional health. Their false beliefs are bolstered by a corporate culture of greed that bottles sex with every product marketed to you. The message: Free sex is fun and available (and something's wrong with you if you feel bad afterward). And, disillusioned by your prospects for real commitment, you may be hedging your bets with years of education and career building that are shrinking your fertility window. But you can't find the right time or the right man to embark on motherhood.

The 30-Day Love Detox is the beginning of your transformation. It will help give you a better perspective on your choices. It will give you some practice in boundary setting. And it will empower you to bravely have the "What are we?" conversation—and move away fast if the answer doesn't support your relationship life plan. This is your life, your eggs, your future. The power is in your hands.

CHAPTER 9

Tech Mating

....

"**T**echnology is the problem," sighed an exasperated young corporate lawyer. She was sitting in my living room, sipping sauvignon blanc and nibbling on olives with a group of single women—all bemoaning the dearth of commitment-oriented single men. "Guys don't call anymore. They just text."

"Or they send Facebook messages," chimed in a TV production assistant. "What's up with that? It's, like, my cell phone and e-mail box are now too *personal*."

They're right, of course. The more distance a man (especially an avoidant one) can put between himself and emotional intimacy, the better for him. And the more secure his electronic leash on you to obtain sex when he thinks he needs it, the happier he is. Technology is his escape hatch and his leash. But tech itself isn't the problem. That would be like saying automobiles cause car accidents. Cars don't cause accidents. *Drivers* do. And in this chapter, you're about to learn how to drive your smartphone into a healthy relationship.

Technology's Loveology

The idea behind this chapter started with a middle school girl. She's what I call a digital native—a kid who was pushing buttons long before she was flushing toilets. As far as love is concerned, she's had only one entire school semester of dating experience under her belt. But her uncanny ability to give a pro like me relationship advice on love's high-tech playing field was almost savantlike.

It happened like this: I was having dinner at a California Pizza Kitchen with three 13-year-old girls when I received a text from a 42-year-old guy I'd been dating for about six weeks.

"Oooh," sang my own daughter in an age-old schoolgirl taunt. "Is that from your *boyfriend*?"

I responded with the defensive girlish quip I perfected 25 years ago: "He's *not* my boyfriend!"

Her friend, the tech savant, immediately took meaning from my response and nodded knowingly. "Oh, then you only text," she said firmly, as if to imply that a texting relationship is indeed a kind of relationship but not one that deserves the title of boyfriend.

Then, I confused her. "No, we talk, too. But only via cell. I haven't given him my home number yet. And we have dinner dates," I said.

I watched her eyes widen as her tech-savvy mind tried to make sense of what I was saying. "Well, is he your Facebook friend?"

"No," I said, "we're not ready for that."

"Does he follow you on Twitter?"

"Nope."

Then, she gave me a look that read "How can you sit at the same lunch table with a boy who isn't even online with you?" It was then that I realized that today, the level of two people's tech infiltration indicates a level of intimacy and, indeed, commitment. If his Facebook friends can't see me, then I'm still not real. I'm only in a little side compartment in his life.

As I thought further about this insight, I began to think more about the collision between our digital world and our relationships. I realized that many people underestimate the value of technology in their relationships. Others overestimate the real-world outcomes and get lost in a fantasy world of digital relationships that produce real emotions but no real boyfriends. I thought about all my older friends who have gone "retrosexual" and searched through online social networks for their first love. By the way, if your friends tell you they haven't done this, they're lying. My own twelfth-grade crush, Carl, isn't even on Facebook. (Don't ask me how I know this!)

I see others being tagged in party pictures that might send prospective mates running for the hills or elicit a very cold shoulder from the current mate at home. And worst of all, I've seen technology infect perfectly healthy humans with a case of Love ADD (attention deficit disorder) as opportunities for new love have expanded around the globe.

Technology seems especially to be the new singles bar for the over-40 set. A recent study from the Oxford Internet Institute found that those in the 40 to 69 age group use dating sites more than their younger single peers do. Slightly more than a third of this group said they had found that special someone on the Internet.[1] Users of American dating sites range in age from 25 to 65; the biggest group is ages

35 to 50.[2] And most are women. Makes sense. In a woman's childbearing years, she has little time to get out of the house because she's likely working and giving care to more than one generation of people.

Plus, the online hunt is apparently fun. A researcher at the University of Missouri School of Journalism used brain sensors to record data while people browsed Facebook. He found that the most pleasure came when users searched for a specific target, such as an old love or a crush from work.[3] And you obviously can't participate in this pleasure without a computer—access to which is something that in itself is linked to romantic success. Another recent study presented by the American Sociological Association showed that more than 80 percent of people with full Internet access were also in a romantic relationship.[4] Go figure.

Back to my digital hookup genius at California Pizza Kitchen. What this middle school girl was really trying to explain to me with her wide-eyed look is that tech is more than a modern-day Cupid. Once Cupid's arrow strikes, technology becomes an extension of our relationships. It helps us research mates for compatibility and protection. Then, it enables us to play out the romantic "chase" with precision by allowing us to control the frequency, duration, and level of contact. It can enhance rapport-building communication (especially helpful when we are attracted to the strong silent type). And it's our public billboard about our relationship status and our watchdog over partners who might be lookers, lurkers, or cheaters.

The Challenge

On the surface, technology is a great solution to relationship confusion. It enables a strategic hunt, a clean capture, and a nice electronic leash for life in couple captivity. But it does have its drawbacks.

Technology was designed to keep us connected. It has morphed into a monster that has millions of people keeping in touch yet touching nothing tender. Fully 95 percent of 18- to 29-year-olds use text messaging on their phones, and these users send or receive an average of 87.7 text messages on a normal day. In fact, 18- to 24-year-olds send or receive an average of 109.5 text messages per day. That works out to more than 3,200 messages per month.[5]

As we discussed in the last chapter, emotional intimacy is the ultimate glue that makes relationships secure, but technological communication is the antithesis of intimate. Take Twitter as a prime example. The text-based megaphone to your contact list limits your feelings to 140 characters or fewer. Including spaces. Unless you're Ernest Hemingway, it's impossible to communicate anything of depth with such brevity.

And texting may be instant, but it's far from intimate. It's a communication void of body language, eye contact, vocal tone, and pheromones. Imagine your favorite band without the drummer or the lead vocalist and you'll understand how inferior text communication is. Even longer messages sent via Facebook or traditional e-mail may be filled with more words but can be seriously lacking in emotional content, especially if one isn't a very good writer. Much emotion is lost in translation from heart to text.

Tech As a Love Tool

With that said, there are plenty of positive ways to use technology to find, grow, and maintain a healthy relationship. And for women in particular, it's a great way to track your attachment behaviors and even train a man to be a more intimate communicator.

"Technology brings us all closer together—across space, time, social class, race, religion, ethnicity," says Sam Yagan, cofounder of OkCupid.com. "We now have opportunities to meet and interact with people outside our neighborhoods and indeed all over the world. But the biggest negative thing is that for some people, digital communication can overly substitute for human interaction. It is meant to augment communication, not replace it."

In the next few pages, I'm going to give you some serious strategies for using technology in your love life—whether you want to increase your statistical probability of finding a real boyfriend online or shape the behavior of a budding boyfriend who texts too much. I'm also going to explain how easy access to online pornography is rewiring men's brains and why he thinks it's okay to ask for naked photos of you. An understanding of the psychology of sexting will make you think twice before you send a suggestive text to a man you don't have a real commitment from. Finally, I'll tell you the ten biggest mistakes women make with technology and love.

We Evolved to Connect

As a species, we're wired to connect. Back in our hunter-gatherer ages, small family groups of humans roamed the land in search of food, shelter, and mates. Some items crucial to our lifelines were extremely scarce in daily life. Thus, we evolved to have an almost insatiable craving for those things. Consider salt, sugar, and saturated fat. We crave them so that if we stumbled across them, we would be quick to relish and devour them.[6] I think we all know that fast-food chains have cashed in on those cravings by filling their menus with items loaded with salt, sugar, and fat. Junk food tastes good, and in the short term, it feels good because its ingredients were once so rare.

But there are two other trace nutrients that humans crave: companionship and sex. Humans don't do well in isolation. Being alone for extended periods of time can cause major psychological pain and even physical symptoms of distress. That's why solitary confinement is a preferred torture by jail guards. And sexual intercourse was and is obviously necessary for the survival of our species. Ages ago, an opportunity to add new genes to the tribe's gene pool was a big treat. If a strange hunter rolled in and he was carrying protein, he was welcomed by many women. In the same way that we've evolved to salivate at the thought of salt, sugar, and fat, we now do the same with opportunities for connectedness and sex.

But we're not in a lonely tribe in the forest anymore. Today, we walk through jam-packed nightclubs, we crush against each other on crowded subways, and we point our computer mouse toward millions of potential mates. In fact, we're more likely to suffer from "friend buildup" than loneliness.

And no longer is sex a rare opportunity. Sex is available everywhere at any time. Finding sex today is no different from finding junk food at every turn.

Our relationships have become junk food relationships. They taste good in the short term but seriously lack emotional nutrition. Like fast food, too many brief junk food relationships make us unhealthy. Online dating sites capitalize on our cravings for connection, but it's up to you to control your own intake. Today's high-supply love economy can make us sick or it can make us healthy. It depends on how we control our cravings.

Finding Love Online

To prepare for this chapter, I looked at the ever-expanding body of research on online behavior and psychology and I had long conversations with two of the hottest innovators in the online dating world. Yagan is the cofounder and chief executive officer of OkCupid.com, the second-largest dating site next to Match.com and the site known for producing an arsenal of statistics about online dating behavior. OkCupid also holds the distinction of being the dating site of choice for artists, hipsters, and people in creative jobs.

Josh Meyers is the CEO of People Media, the largest provider of targeted dating communities, including OurTime .com for singles over 50, BlackPeopleMeet.com (the name says it all), and SingleParentMeet.com. All three sites are number one in their categories.

"With so much mobility and family distancing, people still need to have a network to connect. And online activity brings people together," says Meyers. "Facebook is about keeping track of the people you know. Online dating is about meeting people you don't know. It provides opportunity for a wide range of spouses to meet. Even cities are segregated."

And online dating has come a long way from the days when it had a reputation of being the bastion for creepy shut-ins. Online dating has become mainstream.

"The stigma has been lost," says Yagan. "If you still have a stigma to online dating, then that means you think your friends are weird because they're mostly all doing it."

The second major change is a platform shift. Online dating has moved to wireless devices, and this is allowing for real-time connections. Yes, your smartphone can be used to create instant flash-friends, says Yagan. "Now you can be at home on a Friday night and want to go out and simply tell a group of local single people what bar or restaurant you're headed to," he says. We'll talk about personal security in a minute, but first, let's talk about your personal marketing.

Your Online Sales Pitch

....

Unless you've been living on Mars, you've read enough online profiles today to know which ones look good and which ones would get an F. But OkCupid's online analytics show clear statistics about who gets the hits and who doesn't. For example, men who wear red shirts in their profile photos get more clicks than guys who wear blue. Women who smile get fewer clicks than women who pout. (Yes, that silly duck face.) Shorter women get more clicks than tall women.

And men's profiles are particularly rife with exaggerations and outright lies. Men lie about height, income, and the age of their photos. According to OkCupid's research, the hottest pictures tend to be the oldest. If you see a good-looking picture of a man older than 30 on a dating Web site, that photo is very likely to be outdated.[7] So, even simple basics can increase your chances of finding love. Take a clear, recent photo and spell correctly.

"One of the most surprising facts is that if you take a picture that doesn't use a flash, you can look up to seven years younger," says Yagan. "We advise people to take a picture in the mirror of their bathroom or anywhere in their natural world. Or how about the simple fact that grammar matters? If you don't care about yourself enough to make your profile grammatically correct, how can you care enough about your relationships?"

But Meyers says that online dating behavior based on gender is most fascinating to him.

"I see surprisingly traditional gender roles. Men act as the hunters casting a wide net. They are visually stimulated. They don't read profiles and they send many, many form e-mails. Women, on the other hand, tend to wait to be contacted. They send fewer targeted messages. They fall in love with a specific profile. They read it. They analyze it from ten different angles. They may send one e-mail to a specific guy."

I smiled when he told me that. Are we *that* obvious? What's worse than us being hesitant to hunt is that we think the e-mail a guy sends us was composed specifically for us because he read every detail of our profile. If he comments on specific things we write (not things he noticed in the photos), then you might believe it. But if he talks only about himself and adds your name a couple of times, you've just been cast a hook with a form letter as bait.

Meyers thinks men and women need to adopt each other's practices. "Men should send some thoughtful, targeted messages that are specific. That sends the message they are the only ones. Women shouldn't necessarily chase men with e-mails. That will turn them off. But they should view a lot of profiles without sending a message. Men will know who viewed them and wonder why the women didn't write them. That's interesting to a guy."

He also adds that women should keep track of who viewed their profile so they'll notice a potential suitor's e-mail. Because trust me, if you've never been online before as a woman, you'll be shocked at the confusing range of e-mails you get.

With all the fabrications about lifestyle and photoshopped photos, it can be a little intimidating to just "be yourself" online. But that's the biggest advice Yagan gave me. Being honest also increases your statistical probability that you'll find a true match. (Then, you'll use *The 30-Day Love Detox* to see if that match is interested in sex or in a relationship.)

"The biggest mistake is that people try to be the person that they think most people want," says Yagan. "If you are looking for someone who is really into you, you need to be authentic. Here's an example: There are two women's profiles. One woman scores a seven out of ten by most male users. Another woman scores a one with 70 percent of male users but a ten with 30 percent who like her uniqueness. The second woman will most likely meet a compatible date. Trying to please everyone means that you're not going to passionately energize anyone."

Both dating Web site gurus agree that online dating isn't designed for you to have online *relationships*. The best way to use them is to target someone interesting and move to the real world quickly.

Cautions Meyers: "The longer you keep an e-mail relationship, the disappointment is huge when you finally meet. If one person really likes the person, the first date can feel like a breakup. I think there's value in getting the physical attraction piece confirmed or denied. Sooner is best."

And both CEOs suggest you use the same safety precautions you would in the real world. "If you met a nice stranger on the subway, you wouldn't go into a dark alley with him, but you might join him for a coffee," says Yagan.

For a first date, meet in a public place—maybe a Starbucks—and keep it short. You can meet again, but it's always good to leave them wanting more. The second date will be the actual date because you've now confirmed you're attracted to each other.

Considering our current addiction to dating and our

human craving for companionship and sex, be aware that the opportunity provided by online dating can produce a chronic dater rather than a great long-term mate.

Meyers admits that dating addicts are certainly out there. "You have to go back to what is your goal. What are you trying to achieve? If you want to keep changing companions, there's no reason to back off, but if your goal is to have a family, then you're not doing yourself a service. Do I want to be a serial monogamist? Is this what I want to lead for the rest of my life?"

Online dating is actually quite simple. Make an authentic profile, send only short messages to men, meet quickly (and safely) before your fantasy life takes over, and know who you are and what you want. Then, stick to it. The same rules apply for meeting men in the real world. Becoming an expert at reading into online dating profiles can be a useful activity while you're doing *The 30-Day Love Detox*.

Training a Texter

In my dozens of interviews with single women, one complaint I heard over and over was that men text too much and don't pick up the phone. Some text just to keep in contact but rarely call for dates. Others attempt to maintain all relationship communication via text and meet in the real world—mostly for sex rather than talk.

If a man is left to his own devices (pun intended) and a woman is happy to text him back, this is the pattern that many modern dating relationships settle into. In other words, a road to nowhere. It's simply a text-based holding pattern where the woman wonders about the status of a relationship and holds her breath between encouraging text communication.

But women have far more power than they know. And as when doing the rest of *The 30-Day Love Detox*, women need to be brave and trust that taking control will be perceived as attractive to the right man. In fact, text is a great way to test a man's intentions. It's one of those modern courting rituals I talked about in Chapter 6. Good, commitment-oriented men will put your needs first as a demonstration of their intentions. If he won't call you, he certainly won't marry you.

Training a good man to refrain from texting and to pick up the phone is no different from training a child to stop whining. Bottom line: You simply don't reward the behavior. And at the same time, you reward the behaviors you do like. It stands to reason that he's going to continue to text if you continue to reward him by texting responses to him.

But first, you have to be convinced this is what you want. Like the relationship system strategies that I talked about in the last chapter, you've got be clear with yourself and clear with him. Ambivalence is your enemy. If your worry that he'll leave is stronger than your belief that he'll learn to call, you won't succeed.

The earlier in a relationship you begin his training, the better. A guy you've just met and aren't having sex with will be more motivated to change his style than a guy you've had a text relationship with for nine months. Start by responding to his first (or most recent) text with this text:

> I prefer to use text for quick messages about meeting times and places. I'll try to always pick up my phone when I see your number. ☺

Those two sentences will give him a lot of information about you. First, this text shows you know who you are and that you have boundaries. It also implies you'd like face-to-face contact. And it shows that his phone call will be rewarded with your happy voice. The smiley face shows you aren't angry and that you're open and receptive.

That's the easiest part of the text training. The next part gets a little trickier. Just like a toddler who wants a cookie while a mother is cooking dinner, he'll test you. A toddler will test the rule with whining, tears, and tantrums, and when your back is turned, he or she will make a beeline to the cookie jar. Your dude will do it by continuing to text you.

Perhaps the most common thing a mother finds herself saying to a kid is, "Didn't I just tell you *not* to do that? Why are you doing it?" In fact, a rule isn't a rule until a behavioral consequence has been demonstrated. A mother might have to turn off the stove and walk over to the cookie jar with her arms folded and her face stern. You, on the other hand, have to keep your manicured fingers off your smartphone keys. Don't text back. No matter what he writes. You're setting up a system. He's testing you. You need to be firm. Don't reward him.

After he exhausts himself with friendly, inviting text messages, he'll move to step two and give you the silent treatment. (And if he sent an angry text, you can count your blessings that you screened him out early.) He will go away, lick his wounds, and busy himself with other women who'll text him back. But he'll still be thinking about you. He might wait a week and text again. At this stage, you might respond with only a smiley face emoticon to let him know you're not mad and your phone is still working. But *do not type any words*. He needs to get the message—and call.

The third stage is the phone call, and this is when you get to reward his good behavior. As much as you're angry about his silly game, you're not allowed to inject any sarcasm in your voice. "I see you finally figured out how to work a phone" won't be received well. Instead, pick up after one ring, put a smile in your voice, and simply say, "Hi! How are you? I've been so busy, but I was just thinking about you." He doesn't need to know that even if you were busy, you found time to read and reread all his texts every day and count the hours between each one. That's between you and your therapist. This is the time to gush and make him feel good about picking up the phone. A mother training a toddler might give the child two cookies *after* dinner to reward him or her for waiting. Rewarding good behavior is the most important piece of behavioral shaping.

The cycle might continue. He might think that one phone call was enough and go back to his old ways. Each time, you'll have to retrain him. After you're dating for a while and feel more secure in the relationship, you might begin to use text for what it was intended for with texts like this:

> In a meeting. See you at the theater at seven. XOXO. ☺

Text and Attachment

I believe there's a close link between electronic communication and attachment style. One single man I interviewed told me that if he really likes a woman, he makes sure he calls rather than e-mails. He knows this is a clear way to let her know he's interested in her for more than sex.

But in today's high-supply sexual economy with emotional avoidance reaching epidemic proportions, text,

Facebook, and e-mail are convenient ways to keep a safe distance from intimacy yet still obtain sex. Still, emotional intimacy is the necessary ingredient to spawn a commitment. If you find yourself *preferring* electronic communication, it might be time to think about your own tolerance for closeness and begin to work on that. On the other hand, if men are falling off your radar because they can't pick up the phone, you need to feel relief. As I said in Chapter 7, you don't need the attention of twelve men—just one.

The Porn Effect and Your Sexts

Back in 2009, Simon Louis Lajeunesse, a professor at the School of Social Work at the University of Montreal, launched a study to examine the effects of pornography on men. In order to do sound science, he needed to compare two groups: young men who have consumed pornography and a control group of young men who haven't consumed pornography. There was only one problem. He couldn't find even one man who hadn't used porn.

After amending his research strategies, he instead studied where, how much, and the kinds of porn men consume. Lajeunesse found that 90 percent of pornography is gobbled up on the Internet, while 10 percent still comes from video stores. On average, single men watch pornography three times a week for forty minutes. Those who are in committed relationships watch it on average 1.7 times a week for twenty minutes.[8]

A full 30 percent of all content on the Internet is pornography.[9] That's a lot of naked women being fed digitally to men. And it explains why so many men beg women to text them a naked photo. The computer and the smartphone have become their sources of stimulation.

One 34-year-old male architect I interviewed explained it this way: "It's like my smartphone has become an extension of my sexuality. This thing *is* sex to me. And it's hard now to have sex without an electronic component."

In Mark Regnerus's research on premarital sex in America, he found that when young men were asked if they had to choose between giving up porn or giving up sex with a warm body forever, a shocking number of men couldn't decide.[10]

Men are more likely to use porn alone, and when they use it with a partner, it's often because porn is the only route to an erection.[11] Women watch porn, too, but more often with partners than alone because they use it as a tool to enhance their relationships. Pornography is one of those "cultural stimulants" that has affected women's sexuality, too. It can create a constant environment of sexual response that's tricking women into believing that their sexuality is just like a man's.

This tidal wave of cheap, available, and increasingly violent pornography can cause some major relationship problems. It can hurt emotionally when our men prefer a digital playmate over us, and it can hurt financially when porn becomes addictive. But the biggest problem is that frequent porn use can cause sexual dysfunction in men. Have you ever experienced a sexual encounter when a man seems to keep his erection forever, incessantly plunging until you're on the verge of a bladder infection? It's called *delayed ejaculation*, and it's also a symptom of too much porn. Or he may have delayed ejaculation's cousin: erectile dysfunction. Think of it this way: Men are highly visually stimulated and turned on by new stimuli. A man who spends a good chunk of his sex life jerking off and fantasizing to porn—endless pictures of young, hot, and always different partners—is, over time, likely to find his long-term girlfriend or wife less interesting than that bottomless supply of new and exciting women in his head. Some men have even reported they've begun faking orgasms with real women.[12]

And that's exactly why he wants you to text him a naked picture of yourself. My advice: Don't bite. You'll be discarded as fast as all the women in his catalogue of digital girlfriends. When you send sexy messages or naked photos, he's less likely to be titillated in anticipation of you and more likely to become aroused enough to finish the job himself. In his head, he's had sex with you. The chase is over. Remember Dr. Buss's study on men with many sexual partners? The more partners he's had, the more likely he is to perceive diminished attractiveness in each new partner. Your naked photo is a kind of sex partner for a man who uses porn a lot.

The 30-Day Love Detox is a way to create a different brain stimulation in the right kind of man. You're the one who's different. Your *lack* of a naked photo will tweak his brain—not in a visual way but in a deeper way. If he's at a state of readiness for commitment, he'll sit up and notice. You're what he's looking for.

Cyberporn addicts spend at least eleven or twelve hours per week online[13] (including tablets, smartphones, laptops, and traditional computers), but the amount of time spent can be double or even triple that amount. The sad news for men is that it can take years to overcome a porn addiction and rewire the brain to be able to enjoy the pleasures of a warm body.[14] But make no mistake, participating in porn consumption with him is no different from being an enabler to a drug addict. Don't do it.

The Ten Biggest
Tech Mistakes
Single Women Make

1. DISCLOSING TMI

Women love to disclose too much information via e-mail and text. While it's easier to write something than to say it, a text-based relationship is just a fantasy. It's pretend intimacy if it's void of eye contact, body language, vocal tone, and touch. When you disclose too much emotional material before a relationship is secure, you set yourself up for feelings of shame and disappointment.

2. SEXTING

Many men will try. And about one in four women will comply. But sending a sext is giving the farm away before he's paid for it (with love and commitment).

3. SETTLING FOR TEXT AND E-MAIL OVER PHONE AND FACE TIME

Women need to be brave. Express your needs clearly and kindly. Use the techniques in this chapter for curing his text addiction, and if he moves away, know it's his loss.

4. KEEPING DIGITAL RELATIONSHIPS WITH OTHER MEN

If you're really into him, you needn't keep a backup man around online. And having text and e-mail relationships with other men will decrease your need and ability to secure one intimate attachment.

5. TEXT STALKING THAT ISN'T RECIPROCATED

Women who have an anxious attachment style tend to over-text. If you're sending more texts than he does, take a step back (and maybe you shouldn't be sending any at all).

6. RESPONDING TO A LATE-NIGHT TEXT

The second you respond to a guy who's trolling for a hookup, you've lost. To hold some power in your romantic life and advertise yourself to all the amazing good guys out there, you need to set the hours when you'll respond to men. The good guys will figure it out and call you.

7. FALLING IN LOVE SIGHT UNSEEN

If you've met someone on Facebook, Twitter, or a dating Web site, don't allow yourself to get caught up in a fantasy that they're perfect. Meet soon after the introduction before your emotions get the best of you.

8. SPENDING MONEY ON MEN TOO SOON

The news has been filled with stories of men who swindle high-earning women for money. The scenario goes like this: Two people meet online and have a few dates. The woman falls in love faster (because that's what women do), and the two plan a trip to Paris or Hawaii. Once they get there, his credit card is mysteriously declined. He's full of apologies and insists it's an error with his bank. She's already in love and in lust and, at this point, hell-bent on having a fabulous romantic vacation. So, she pays for the entire trip. Upon their return, he hightails it for another online target. I'm sorry to say this happens all the time.

9. CHANGING YOUR RELATIONSHIP STATUS TOO SOON

I know you're in love. I know you think he's the best thing since sliced bread, but you can't publicly announce that until you have an agreement with him that the two of you are exclusive. More than a few men have told me that women have changed their Facebook relationship status to "in a relationship" in the early stages of dating. And it made them run for the hills.

10. USING PUBLIC POSTS TO VENT ABOUT EX-BOYFRIENDS

You don't want to look jilted and angry. You don't want to air dirty laundry on social networks. Save all your slander about ex-boyfriends for lunch with a girlfriend.

As fast as I type this, technology is advancing. I hear the upcoming iPhone has a virtual hologram projector! But the psychology remains the same. If you shouldn't send a sext or a naked photo, you certainly shouldn't send a naked

> "Trying to please everyone means that you're not going to passionately energize anyone."
> —OkCupid cofounder Sam Yagan

hologram. A healthy relationship doesn't require cheap substitutions for intimacy or sex. I promise you, there are so many wonderful, commitment-oriented men out there. They just need you to use your feminine power to help them. You're the guardian of the social order, and the controller of the technology is your hand. Use the power wisely, cavewoman.

CHAPTER 10

Survival of the Smartest

I was in a bathroom stall at the Pentagon. My fingers were shaking as I fumbled to connect the parts of a portable breast pump. I'd had better highs in bathroom stalls, but I believe this was my defining moment as a woman.

Up until then, I thought I'd done everything my culture told me to achieve female success. I'd become highly educated. I'd become flexible to satisfy a mobile workforce. I was physically fit with a Stairmaster butt that rivaled a bathing suit model's. I had great clothes and could do everything a man could do—all in five-inch heels. I'd even proudly had a baby out of wedlock because I could afford it. And I'd been able to ignore my churning new-mother stomach and hop on a plane for a

TV assignment. Because that's what successful women are supposed to do. But still, I couldn't get that darned breast pump together!

The problem wasn't mechanical or physical. It was nerves. I'd been in Washington, DC, for twenty hours, and the separation from my three-month-old infant surprisingly jumbled my thoughts and rattled my core. Ironically, I was there to champion female freedom. I was assigned to interview the highest-ranking woman in the United States military—a three-star general whose long dedication to her career had been rewarded in the most male of arenas: the Army. But while I was waiting for her holiness to arrive, I felt my swollen breasts begin a trickle that slowly wet my blouse. No worries. I could handle this. Buttoning my blazer, I stood up and asked politely if there was a restroom nearby. As the general's secretary mentally debated whether I had security clearance, the trickle down my chest silently became a torrent. Eventually, she decided I required armed escorts to accompany me and picked up the phone to summon a couple. By the time I reached that bathroom stall, my blouse was soaked, my hands were shaking, and I wondered what kind of lethal contraption the armed soldiers outside my door imagined I was assembling.

But my moment of truth didn't fully hit until the end of the interview when I asked Claudia Kennedy, a 51-year-old retired army lieutenant general with three tours overseas under her belt, what her biggest regret in life had been. Without pausing to reflect, she simply stated she regretted not having experienced motherhood.

That was it. The seal of approval from the Queen herself. By the time my taxi arrived, we had a laugh over my breast-pumping story and I showed her baby pictures. And when I landed back in Los Angeles, I resolved to never, ever fly away from a nursing baby again—no matter what it cost me. I found my hard boundary. Don't mess with my baby!

Don't Mess with My Heart!

....

I'll admit it: I'm a slow learner. Not when it comes to acquiring academic information and passing silly information tests. I'm slow when it comes to setting boundaries. Frankly, I tried to please too many people for too long. And I was very slow when it came to learning to set boundaries with and make demands of men. The needs of a vulnerable infant taught me how to be strong. And I want to show you how you can take a mother's protective "Don't mess with my kid!" mentality and apply it to your vulnerable heart.

Being brave enough to go against your culture, your media, and your peers is what it takes to create a healthy relationship in a high-supply sexual economy.

It's no different from how I choose to parent in a culture that doesn't support natural motherhood. I listened to my body and my innate cavewoman wisdom and I nursed each of my children for three years. Yep, I was a Dairy Queen for six years. (That young mother breastfeeding her three-year-old on the cover of *Time* magazine last Mother's Day was so yesterday!) And I negotiated business contracts to include shorter work hours, higher pay, and limited travel. I was even able to negotiate one deal where any business trip had to include an extra plane ticket for my lap baby and nanny so it wouldn't affect my breast milk supply. (I'll always love you, CNET!) I didn't get much of a pushback because, like the former virgin I interviewed, I was so resolved inside myself about what was right for me that my negotiations were pleasant, firm, and easy.

This is what you'll find when you become sure within yourself about your relationship plan. Negotiating with men for care and commitment will become easy once you're convinced that you deserve it. And that may be the hard part: convincing yourself that you deserve fidelity, exclusivity, and an emotionally intimate relationship. And once you're convinced, the next important thing is to negotiate with the right man.

One of the ways we protect ourselves from a terrifying intimate relationship is to seek it from the wrong partner and then conveniently blame him for the aftermath. If you find yourself constantly male bashing, you've got to also ask yourself why you gambled your heart and your bloodstream on a poor bet. Granted, many men lie. In fact, "I love you" is the most common lie men use to obtain sex.[1] So it's up to you to discern his intentions. Sex is a much higher risk for you—for STDs, pregnancy, and a broken heart. And you have a fertility window he simply doesn't have. Using *The 30-Day Love Detox* will help you begin to look for the select kind of man—and there are millions out there— who can offer kindness and commitment.

In all my interviews with young women, the most common thing I hear is "It's too early. I want to just have fun in my twenties." This is one of the most dangerous narratives for women who eventually want a committed relationship and/or motherhood. If you subscribe to this philosophy, I want to speak directly to you. Not only are you training yourself for frequent short-term, low-criteria relationships, but you're ignoring the fact that some of your smart peer women are closing deals all around you and shrinking the pool of eligible men. If you wait too long, the game gets harder and harder to win. Motherhood may not always be an option for you. Surprisingly, research shows that when young women become mothers in college, graduate school, or at the beginning of their careers, the toll on their careers is much less than if they take a break in the middle.[2] And remember, the peak of female fertility is about age 20.[3]

It's spring as I write this. Graduation season. Yesterday, I saw a heartwarming TV news story that depicted a college graduation ceremony. As one young female graduate climbed the stairs to accept her diploma, her boyfriend (a fellow graduate) jumped on stage, went down on one knee, and held up a box with a ring. The crowd went wild. The young woman jumped up and down, grabbed her diploma and that ring, and did a championship dance. She had won both games.

I Didn't See It Coming

It's not surprising I "ended up" as a single mother. Like you, the deck was stacked against me. I was busy with schooling and working and dating. Somehow, my twenties and most of my thirties slipped by. All the time I was thinking I was making personal choices, my culture kept my best options a secret. No one ever told me that motherhood could be the most meaningful achievement ever. That the tears I'd shed at school holiday pageants trumped any workplace accolade. And no one told me that so many men would quit their jobs as providers/protectors. And for sure they didn't tell me that my fun sex life was training my peer men for long-term bachelorhood.

The research is shocking. Everything we're told to do directly impedes our chances for a healthy relationship and motherhood. If you're a woman who's educated, earns a good income, and is well traveled, open-minded, and physically attractive, you're the least likely to be married, divorce free, and a mother.

Education and career advancement introduce women to a smaller pool of like-minded single men and use a big chunk of our fertility years. Being well traveled and having lived in different places trains us for breakups rather than commitment.[4] Having open-minded, liberal attitudes makes you less likely to marry early enough to have children. (Conservatives get married a lot, but they also divorce more. Liberals wait to get married, so they don't have as much time for as many divorces.) Being physically attractive—whether your good looks came from Mother Nature or a gym and the cosmetics industry—exposes you to more sexual opportunities and makes you more inclined to divorce.[5]

Now don't get me wrong. I'm not proposing for one minute that women scale back their career ambitions, get less education, or let their health and beauty go. What I'm saying in the only stone-cold way this former *Sex and the City* babe can say it is that if you leave your relationships to chance, chances are you'll lose.

If my wake up call was alerted out of a desire to protect my children and do what's best for them, I'm wondering if you could do the same for your heart? (Or perhaps even your eggs?) A relationship is a home for the heart, and early sex in multiple relationships sets your heart up for a life of homelessness. Knowing your own love style is just the beginning. Next comes the creation of a firm relationship plan with a timeline and clear goal. The dirty word in *The 30-Day Love Detox* is *if.* You can't say "if" it happens. Adopt an attitude of "when" it will happen, and then date men on a similar timeline.

It's really simple to call the shots and feel your power once you've identified your goal and your target. The men most likely to marry are educated, have high intelligence that gives them the muscles of monogamy, were raised with some religion, have good relationships with their parents, have siblings who are marrying, and have reached their state of readiness. Throwing yourself at a low-criteria man in hopes you'll change him will rarely work.

Psychotherapist Meg Jay, PhD, reminds us that committed relationships are also bridges between families and that families are the best places to raise children. When you're dating him, you might also be checking out the availability of his parents. Grandparents are crucial. Trust me, there may well come a postpartum day when you're simultaneously recovering from a C-section incision, two cracked nipples, and a serious case of pregnancy hemorrhoids—and his *mother* will be far more important to you than him. And you'll wish you had dated her first.

A Voice for Fourteen Million Single Mothers

It was like a scene out of a reality TV show. The night before had been a rough single mother night. Both my daughters and I were down with a stomach flu that made the movie *The Exorcist* look tidy, and the little one had a painful ear infection to boot. My extended family lives in Canada, not LA, so in a moment of desperation, I broke down and called my ex. He talked my whining daughter down off the ledge and promised her that "Daddy would come by after work." But he was a no-show.

By 8:00 a.m., the kids had soiled every sheet and towel in the house, and I had to leave my angels alone to run to the cleaners—there was just too much for my home washing machine. So, there I was—my hair in a greasy knot, in stained gray sweats, with circles under my eyes, carting four huge trash bags full of barfy linens. And in he sails. Gliding smoothly from his sparkling clean Range Rover in a crisp shirt and tie, fresh from the gym. He takes one look at me, says nothing, grabs his clean shirts, and runs out like an Olympic gold medalist. Single ladies, these are the men you're rewarding with sex.

The good news is we all recovered. And I love to laugh and tell that story over wine with all my single mom girlfriends. Seriously, that man booted out of that dry cleaners like he'd just seen a ghost. My kids are thriving today. My oldest went to Stanford's program for gifted youth last summer, and my daughter with Asperger's syndrome is a competitive cheerleader and fashion genius. I call her my Fashion-Aspie. Every choice I make in my life gets weighed against the impact on my girls. So, for now, I don't date. I prefer to use my valuable time to be a mother, a father, a protector, a provider, and a nurturer. And to keep my children safe from any bad choice I might make. But there will be time again for love. My oldest will be in college in just three years, so watch out. I'm coming back! Yes, I believe women can have it all—just not all at the same time.

And my rules about putting motherhood before work haven't changed. Instead, they get noticed and rewarded by men and women in corporate America who understand. Before Dr. Phil hired me to participate in his spin-off show *The Doctors*, he asked me why I had taken such a big "break" from my TV career. I told him I'd been unprepared for the overwhelming desire to nurture and I just couldn't leave my kids when they were young. As a father (and now doting grandfather!), he totally got that.

I once interrupted a business meeting at a major New York publisher to do a FaceTime chat with my kids in LA to catch them before they went to school. And the editor I interrupted? She's the bright young woman at Rodale who saw potential in my book and decided to publish it. My "rudeness" in the meeting was apparently overlooked because she could see I stand behind my message.

And my message is simple: Women, you're finally free. The work of your great-grandmothers, grandmothers, and mothers has paved the way to endless choices for you. But nothing is truly free in life. Every decision you make will have consequences—some good, some bad. And it's those consequences I want you to consider. I know it's hard to imagine what you'll want in ten years, but *The 30-Day Love Detox* will help keep more options open and available to you.

Don't forget that you're driving some pretty precious female biology. You fall in love hard and you manufacture spectacular humans. Even my idol, Lieutenant General Claudia Kennedy, couldn't hide from her biology. Two years after my visit to her Pentagon office, I read that she had filed a complaint against another high-ranking officer for sexual harassment. You go, girl! Risking your career to speak out and protect the rights of all women. But the best news of all? The army who had supported her for three decades didn't let her down. They had her back.

The offender was asked to take an early retirement. And rumor has it that President Obama even considered her early on as a running mate for vice president. The general got motherhood anyway. She's nurturing our culture. Thanks, Mom.

Endnotes

....

CHAPTER 1

1   Williams, J. C. (2010). *Reshaping the work-family debate: Why men and class matter.* Cambridge, MA: Harvard University Press.

2   U.S. Centers for Disease Control and Prevention (2010). *Sexually transmitted diseases.* Retrieved from http://www.cdc.gov/std.

3   Coontz, S. (2011). Book review: "The richer sex" on contemporary women by Liza Mundy. *Huffington Post.* Retrieved from http://www.washingtonpost.com/entertainment/books/book-review-the-richer-sex-on-contemporary-women-by-liza-mundy/2012/02/29/gIQA8IqMWS_story.html.

4   Organisation for Economic Co-operation and Development. (2011). *Children in Families.* Retrieved from http://www.oecd.org/dataoecd/62/27/41919533.pdf.

5   Pew Research Center. (2011). *A tale of two fathers: More are active, but more are absent.* Retrieved from http://www.pewsocialtrends.org/2011/06/15/a-tale-of-two-fathers.

6   Bradshaw, C., Kahn, A. S., & Saville, B. K. (2010). To hook up or date: Which gender benefits? *Sex Roles,* 62(9–10), 661–669.

7   Tartakovsky, M. (2008). Depression and anxiety among college students. *Psych Central.* Retrieved from http://psychcentral.com/lib/2008/depression-and-anxiety-among-college-students.

8   Cohen, E. (2007). CDC: Antidepressants most prescribed drugs in U.S. Retrieved from http://articles.cnn.com/2007-07-09/health/antidepressants_1_antidepressants-high-blood-pressure-drugs-psychotropic-drugs?_s=PM:HEALTH.

9   Storrs, C. (2011). Is love better for men's or women's health? Retrieved from http://foxnews.com/imag/Wellness/Is+Love+Better+For+Men's+or+Women's+Health%#F.

10 National Center for Health Statistics. (2009). *Changing patterns of nonmarital childbirth in the United States.* Retrieved from http://www.cdc.gov/nchs/data/databriefs/db18.pdf.

11 Pew Research Center. (2011). *Women see value and benefits of college: Men lag on both fronts survey finds.* Retrieved from http://www. pewsocialtrends.org/2011/08/17/women-see-value-and-benefits-of-college-men-lag-on-both-fronts-survey-finds/4.

12 Mulligan, C. B. (2010). In historical first women outnumber men on U.S. payrolls. Retrieved from http://economix.blogs.nytimes.com/ 2010/02/05/in-historical-first-women-outnumber-men-on-us-payrolls.

13 U.S. Census Bureau. (2011). Education and synthetic work-life earnings estimates. Retrieved from http://www.census.gov/ prod/2011pubs/acs-14.pdf.

14 Domenico, D. M., & Jones, K. H. (2006). Career aspirations of women in the 20th century. *Journal of Career and Technical Education,* 22(2), 3–7.

15 (2001). Prostitution in the Victorian Era (1830-1901). Retrieved from http://everything2.com/title/Prostitution+in+the+Victorian+Era.

16 University of Michigan. (2009). When young men are scarce, they're more likely to play the field than to propose. *ScienceDaily.* Retrieved from http://www. *ScienceDaily.*com /releases/2009/06/090609220829.htm.

17 Hymowitz, K. S. (2011). *Manning up: How the rise of women has turned men into boys.* New York: Basic Books.

18 Pew Research Center. (2010). Women, men, and the new economics of marriage. Retrieved from http://www.pewsocialtrends. org/2010/01/19/women-men-and-the-new-economics-of-marriage.

19 Penn, Schoen & Berland Associates. (2012). Harlequin Romance Report. Retrieved from http://www.harlequin.com/media/images/ pdf/carinapress/2012SurveyFindingsFactSheet.pdf.

20 Easton, J. A., Confer, J. C., Goetz, C. D., & Buss, D. M. (2010). Reproduction expediting: Sexual motivations, fantasies, and the ticking biological clock. *Personality and Individual Differences,* 49(5), 516–520.

21 Pew Research Center. (2010). *Childlessness up among all women: Down among women with advanced degrees.* Retrieved from http:// www.pewsocialtrends.org/2010/06/25/childlessness-up-among-all-women-down-among-women-with-advanced-degrees.

22 Ibid.

23 Cannold, L. (2005). *What, no baby?: Why women are losing the freedom to mother, and how they can get it back.* Fremantle, Western Australia: Curtin University Books.

24 Fertile Hope. (2012). Retrieved from http://www.fertilehope.org/ learn-more/cancer-and-fertility-info/parenthood-options-men.cfm.

25 Connolly, M. P., Hoorens, S., & Chambers, G. M. (2010). The costs and consequences of assisted reproductive technology: An economic perspective. *Human Reproductive Update,* 16(6), 603–613.

26 U.S. Centers for Disease Control and Prevention. (2010). *Assisted Reproductive Technology.* Retrieved from http://www.cdc.gov/art.

27 South, S. J., & Trent, K. (1988). Sex ratios and women's roles: A cross-national analysis. *American Journal of Sociology,* 93(5), 1096–1115.

CHAPTER 2

1 Yamner, G. (2011). The real agenda: Women as second-class citizens. Retrieved from http://www.rhrealitycheck.org/reader-diaries/ 2011/03/28/real-agenda-women-second-class-citizens.

2 Ali, M. (2009, October 2). The traceless warrior. Retrieved from http://tracelesswarrior.blogspot.com/2009/10/eating-bambi.html.

3 Kim, P., Leckman, J.F., Mayes, L.C., Feldman, R., Wang, X., & Swain, J.E. (2010). The plasticity of human maternal brain: longitudinal changes in brain anatomy during the early postpartum period. *Behavioral Neuroscience,* 124(5), 695.

4 Zeigler-Hill, V., & Myers, E. M. (2011). An implicit theory of self-esteem: The consequences of perceived self-esteem for romantic desirability. *Evolutionary Psychology,* 9(2), 147–180.

5 Wedekind, C., & Füri, S. (1997). Body odour preferences in men and women: Do they aim for specific MHC combinations or simply heterozygosity? *Proceedings of the Royal Society of London Series B,* 264: 1471–1479.

6 Alvergne, A., & Lummaa, V. (2009). Does the contraceptive pill alter mate choice in humans? *Trends in Ecology and Evolution,* 25(3), 171–179.

7 Hrdy, S. B. (2009). *Mothers and others: The evolutionary origins of mutual understanding.* Cambridge, MA: Harvard University Press.

8 Dahlberg, F. (1975). *Woman the gatherer.* London: Yale University Press.

9 Biesele, M., & Barclay, S. (2001). Ju/'Hoan women's tracking knowledge and its contribution to their husbands' hunting success. *African Study Monographs,* 26, 67–84.

10 Massachusetts Institute of Technology. (2010). Collective intelligence: Number of women in group linked to effectiveness in solving difficult problems. *ScienceDaily.* Retrieved from http://www. sciencedaily.com /releases/2010/09/100930143339.htm.

11 Kuhn, S. L., & Stiner, M. C. (2006). What's a mother to do? *Current Anthropology,* 47(6), 953–980.

12 Sahlins, M. (1972). *Stone age economics*. Chicago, IL: Aldine-Atherton.

13 Friedan, B. (1963). *The feminine mystique*. New York: Norton.

14 Schneider, D. (2011). Wealth and the marital divide. *American Journal of Sociology*, 117(2), 627–667.

15 DeBell, M. (2008). Children living without their fathers: Population estimates and indicators of educational well-being. *Social Indicators Research*, 87(3), 427–443.

16 U.S. Department of Health and Human Services. (January 2010). *National incidence study of child abuse and neglect (NIS-4) report to Congress*. Retrieved from http://www.acf.hhs.gov/programs/opre/abuse_neglect/natl_incid/reports/natl_incid/nis4_report_congress_full_pdf_jan2010.pdf.

17 Loyola University Health System. (2009). Cupid's arrow may cause more than just sparks to fly this Valentine's Day. *ScienceDaily*. Retrieved from http://www.sciencedaily.com /releases/2009/02/090214104322.htm.

18 Ibid.

19 Förster, J., Epstude, K., & Özelsel, A. (2009). Why love has wings and sex has not: How reminders of love and sex influence creative and analytic thinking. *Personality and Social Psychology Bulletin*, 35(11), 1479–1491.

20 Waite, L. J., & Gallagher, M. (2010). The case for marriage: Why married people are happier, healthier, and better off financially. *Psych Page*. Retrieved from http://www.psychpage.com/family/library/brwaitgalligher.html.

21 Hollander, D. (1997). *101 lies men tell women*. New York: Harper Perennial.

22 Campbell, A. (2008). Attachment, aggression and affiliation: The role of oxytocin in female social behavior. *Biological Psychology*, 77(1), 1–10.

23 University of Nebraska at Lincoln (2011). When it comes to college hookups, more is said than done. *ScienceDaily*. Retrieved from http://www.sciencedaily.com/releases/2011/09/110914143632.htm.

24 Reiber, C., & Garcia, J. R. (2010). Hooking up: Gender differences, evolution, and pluralistic ignorance. *Journal of Evolutionary Psychology*, 8(3), 390–404.

25 Associated Press. (2007). More U.S. women dying in childbirth. Retrieved from http://www.msnbc.msn.com/id/20427256/ns/health-pregnancy/t/more-us-women-dying-childbirth.

26 U.S. Centers for Disease Control and Prevention (2010). *Sexually transmitted diseases*. Retrieved from http://www.cdc.gov/std/herpes/stdfact-herpes.htm.

27 NYU Medical Center. (2009). Women and HIV/AIDS. Retrieved from http://www.hivinfosource.org/hivis/hivbasics/women/index.html.

28 Martin, J. A., Hamilton, B. E., Ventura, S. J., Menacker, F., Park, M. M., & Sutton, P. D. (2002). Births: Final data for 2001. *National Vital Statistics Reports*, 51(2).

29 DeBell, M. (2008). Children living without their fathers: Population estimates and indicators of educational well-being. *Social Indicators Research*, 87(3), 427–443.

CHAPTER 3

1 Ackerman, D. (2012, March 24). The brain on love. *New York Times*. Retrieved from http://opinionator.blogs.nytimes.com/2012/03/24/the-brain-on-love.

2 Grello, C. M., Welsh, D. P., & Harper, M.S. (2006). No strings attached: The nature of casual sex in late adolescents. *The Journal of Sex Research,* 43, 255–267.

3 Busby, D. M., Carroll, J. S., & Willoughby, B. J. (2010). Compatibility or restraint? The effects of sexual timing on marriage relationships. *Journal of Family Psychology,* 24(6), 766–774.

4 Mundy, L. (2012). *The richer sex: How the new majority of female breadwinners is transforming sex, love, and family.* New York: Simon & Schuster.

5 Fraley, R. C., Waller, N. G., & Brennan, K. A. (2000). An item response theory analysis of self-report measures of adult attachment. *Journal of Personality and Social Psychology,* 78, 350–365.

6 Johnson, S. M., & Whiffen, V. E. (2003). *Attachment processes in couples and family therapy.* New York: The Guilford Press.

7 Segal, J., & Jaffe, J. (2012). Attachment and adult relationships: How the attachment bond shapes adult relationships. *Helpguide.* Retrieved from http://www.helpguide.org/mental/eqa_attachment_bond.htm.

8 Solomon, M. F, & Siegel, D. J. (2003). *Healing trauma: Attachment, mind, body, and brain.* New York: Norton.

9 Renegerus, M., & Uecker, J. (2011). *Premarital sex in America: How young Americans meet, mate, and think about marrying.* New York: Oxford University Press.

10 Gillath, O., & Schachner, D. A. (2006). Sex and love: Goals, motives, and strategies: How do sexuality and attachment interact? In M. Mikulincer & G. S. Goodman (Eds.), *Dynamics of romantic love: Attachment, caregiving, and sex.* (pp. 121–147). New York: Guilford Press.

11 Ibid.

12 Ibid.

13 Reiber, C., & Garcia, J. R. (2010). Hooking up: Gender differences, evolution, and pluralistic ignorance. *Evolutionary Psychology,* 8(3), 390–404.

14 University of Iowa. (2010). "Hookups" can turn into meaningful relationships, study suggests. *ScienceDaily.* Retrieved from www.sciencedaily.com/releases/2010/08/100823185415.htm.

15 Corcoran, K., & Fischer, J. (2000). *Measures for clinical practice: A sourcebook (Vol. 1).* New York: The Free Press.

CHAPTER 4

1   Jaeger, C. (2012). The Knot releases 2011 real wedding survey (18,000 brides/grooms participate). *Wedding Business Today.* Retrieved from http://www.weddingbusinesstoday.com/wedding-industry-statistics/the-knot-releases-2011-real-wedding-survey-18000-bridesgrooms-participate.

2   Rice University. (2011). Does Cupid play politics? That "something special" might be your mate's political ideology. *ScienceDaily.* Retrieved from http://www.sciencedaily.com/releases/2011/05/110510151221.htm.

3   Klofstad, K. A., McDermott, R., & Hatemi, P. K. (2011). Do bedroom eyes wear political glasses? The role of politics in human mate attraction. *Evolution and Human Behavior,* 33(2), 100–108.

4   Lauer, R., & Lauer, J. (1986). Factors in long-term marriage. *Journal of Family Issues,* 7(4), 382–390.

5   Buehler, C., & O'Brien, M. (2011). Mothers' part-time employment: Associations with mother and family well-being. *Journal of Family Psychology,* 25(6), 895–906.

6   Morrissey, T. W., Dunifon, R. E., & Kalil, A. (2011). Maternal employment, work schedules, and children's body mass index. *Child Development,* 82(1), 66–81.

7   George Mason University. (2007). Married men really do do less housework than live-in boyfriends. *ScienceDaily.* Retrieved from http://www.sciencedaily.com/releases/2007/08/070827174300.htm.

8   University of Michigan. (2008). Exactly how much housework does a husband create? *ScienceDaily*. Retrieved from http://www. sciencedaily.com/releases/2008/04/080403191009.htm.

9   Huang, P. M., Smock, P. J., Manning, W. D., & Bergstrom-Lynch, C. A. (2011). He says, she says: Gender and cohabitation. *Journal of Family Issues, 32*(7), 876–905.

10 Bindley, K. (2011). National Marriage Project: "Why marriage matters" study says cohabitating parents do kids harm. *Huffington Post*. Retrieved from http://www.huffingtonpost.com/2011/08/20/ national-marriage-project_n_931974.html.

11 Garrison, M. (2008). Reviving marriage: Could we? Should we? *Journal of Law and Family Studies, 10*(2), 279–335.

12 Associated Press. (1987). Divorce may be the price of living together first. *New York Times*. Retrieved from http://www.nytimes.com/ 1987/12/07/us/divorce-may-be-the-price-of-living-together-first.html.

13 Lichter, D. T., & Qian, Z. (2008). Serial cohabitation and the marital life course. *Journal of Marriage and Family, 70*(4), 861–878.

14 Miller, A. J., Sassler, S., & Kusi-Appouh, D. (2011). The specter of divorce: Views from working- and middle-class cohabitors. *Family Relations, 60*(5), 602–616.

15 Jamison, T. B., & Ganong, L. (2011). "We're not living together": Stayover relationships among college-educated emerging adults. *Journal of Social and Personal Relationships, 28*(4), 536–557.

16 University of Missouri at Columbia. (2011). Trend in young adults' dating habits, committed relationships may not lead to marriage. *ScienceDaily*. Retrieved from http://www.sciencedaily.com/ releases/2011/07/110725190040.htm.

17 Parker-Pope, T. (2010). Is marriage good for your health? *New York Times*. Retrieved from http://www.nytimes.com/2010/04/18/ magazine/18marriage-t.html?pagewanted=all.

CHAPTER 5

1   Karolinska Institute. (2008). Infidelity gene? Genetic link to relationship difficulties found. *ScienceDaily*. Retrieved from http://www.sciencedaily.com/releases/2008/09/080902161213.htm.

2   NPR staff. (2009). Battle of the sexes: When women outearn men. NPR. Retrieved from http://www.npr.org/2012/03/18/148677267/ the-battle-of-the-sexes-when-women-out-earn-men.

3   Barber, N. (1995). The evolutionary psychology of physical attractive-
     ness: Sexual selection and human morphology. *Ethology and
     Sociobiology,* 16, 395–424.

4   Buss, D. M. (1994). *The evolution of desire: Strategies of human
     mating.* New York: Basic Books.

5   University of Abertay Dundee (2010). George Clooney Effect?
     High-earning women want older, more attractive partners, research
     finds. *ScienceDaily.* Retrieved from http://www.sciencedaily.com/
     releases/2010/12/101210075920.htm.

6   University of Nebraska at Lincoln. (2011). Do US men value
     fatherhood over their careers? *ScienceDaily.* Retrieved from http://
     www.sciencedaily.com/releases/2011/10/111013113816.htm.

7   Springer (2007). Men choose romance over success. *ScienceDaily.*
     Retrieved from http://www.sciencedaily.com/releases/2007/
     08/070828110650.htm.

8   Binghamton University. (2010). Propensity for one-night stands,
     uncommitted sex could be genetic, study suggests. *ScienceDaily.*
     Retrieved from http://www.sciencedaily.com/releases/2010/12/
     101201095601.htm.

9   Atwood, J. D., & Schwartz, L. (2002). Cyber-sex: The new affair
     treatment considerations. *Journal of Couple & Relationship Therapy:
     Innovations in Clinical and Educational Interventions,* 1(3), 37–56.

10   Mark, K. P., Janssen, E., & Milhausen, R. R. (2011). Infidelity in
     heterosexual couples: Demographic, interpersonal, and personality-
     related predictors of extradyadic sex. *Archives of Sexual Behavior,*
     40(5), 971–982.

11   University of Montreal. (2008). Infidelity dissected: New research on
     why people cheat. *ScienceDaily.* Retrieved from http://www.
     sciencedaily.com/releases/2008/09/080908185238.htm.

12   Black, R. (2010). Smart men less likely than dumb ones to cheat on
     lovers: study. *New York Daily News.* Retrieved from http://articles.
     nydailynews.com/2010-03-02/entertainment/27057710_1_iqs-
     monogamy-smart-men.

13   Mattingly, B. A., Wilson, K., Clark, E. M., Bequette, A. W., &
     Weidler, D. J. (2010). Foggy faithfulness: Relationship quality,
     religiosity, and the perceptions of dating infidelity scale in an adult
     sample. *Journal of Family Issues,* 31, 1465–1480.

14   Lammers, J., Stoker, J. I., Jordan, J., Pollmann, M., & Stapel, D. A.
     (2011). Power increases infidelity among men and women. *Psycho-
     logical Science,* 22(9), 1191–1197.

15   Ibid.

16 American Sociological Association (2010). Men more likely to cheat if they are economically dependent on their female partners, study finds. *ScienceDaily*. Retrieved from http://www.sciencedaily.com/releases/2010/08/100816095617.htm.

17 Etxebarria, I., Ortiz, M. J., Conejero, S., & Pascual, A. (2009). Intensity of habitual guilt in men and women: differences in interpersonal sensitivity and the tendency towards anxious-aggressive guilt. *Spanish Journal of Psychology,* 12(2), 540–554.

18 Northwestern University. (2011). Fathers wired to provide offspring care: Study confirms that testosterone drops steeply after baby arrives. *ScienceDaily*. Retrieved from http://www.sciencedaily.com / releases/2011/09/110912152901.htm.

19 Oregon State University. (2011). Fatherhood can help change a man's bad habits. *ScienceDaily*. Retrieved from http://www.sciencedaily.com/releases/2011/11/111107161800.htm.

20 Regnerus, M., & Uecker, J. (2011). *Premarital sex in America: How you Americans meet, mate, and think about marrying.* New York: Oxford University Press.

21 U.S. Conference of Mayors. (2000). A status report on hunger and homelessness in American cities. Retrieved from http://www.usmayors.org.

22 Youth Villages. (2012). In child sexual abuse, strangers aren't the greatest danger, experts say. *ScienceDaily*. Retrieved from http://www.sciencedaily.com/releases/2012/04/120413100854.htm.

23 Anderson, J. R. (2000). *Learning and memory: An integrated approach* (2nd ed.). New York: John Wiley & Sons.

CHAPTER 6

1 Phillips, J. (2006). *James Tiptree, Jr.: The double life of Alice B. Sheldon.* New York: St. Martin's Press.

2 Zernike, K. (2011, March 21). Gains, and drawbacks, for female professors. *New York Times*. Retrieved from http://www.nytimes.com/2011/03/21/us/21mit.html?scp=1&sq=March%2021,%202011%20female%20professor&st=cse.

3 Jayson, S. (2011, March 30). More college "hookups," but more virgins, too. *USA Today*. Retrieved from http://www.usatoday.com/news/health/wellness/dating/story/2011/03/More-hookups-on-campuses-but-more-virgins-too/45556388/1.

4 Holman, A., & Sillars, A. (2011). Talk about "hooking up": The influence of college student social networks on nonrelationship sex. *Health Communication,* 27(2), 205–216.

5   Jayson. (2011, March 30). *USA Today.*

6   Holman & Sillars. (2011). *Health Communication,* 27(2), 205–216.

7   Peplau, L. A., & Garnets, L. D. (2000). A new paradigm for understanding women's sexuality and sexual orientation. *Journal of Social Issues,* 56(2), 330–350.

8   Meana, M. (2010). Elucidating women's (hetero)sexual desire: definitional challenges and content expansion. *Journal of Sex Research,* 47, 104–122.

9   Maslow, A. H. (1943). A theory of human motivation. *Psychological Review,* 50(4), 370–396.

10 Regnerus, M., & Uecker, J. (2011). *Premarital sex in America: How you Americans meet, mate, and think about marrying.* New York: Oxford University Press.

11 Haselton, M. G., & Buss, D. M. (2001). The affective shift hypothesis: The functions of emotional changes following sexual intercourse. *Personal Relationships,* 8, 357–369.

12 University of Iowa. (2010). "Hookups" can turn into meaningful relationships, study suggests. *ScienceDaily.* Retrieved from http://www.sciencedaily.com/releases/2010/08/100823185415.htm.

13 Regnerus & Uecker. (2011). *Premarital sex in America.*

14 Ibid.

15 Oregon State University. (2011, January 18). Young couples can't agree on whether they have agreed to be monogamous. *ScienceDaily.* Retrieved from http://www.sciencedaily.com/releases/2011/01/110118123554.htm.

16 Metts, S. (2004). First sexual involvement in romantic relationships: An empirical investigation of communicative framing, romantic beliefs, and attachment orientation in the passion turning point. In J. H. Harvey, A. Wenzel, & S. Sprecher (Eds.), *The handbook of sexuality in close relationships* (pp. 135–158). Hillsdale, NJ: Lawrence Erlbaum Associates.

17 Lambert, T. A., Kahn, A. S., & Apple, K. J. (2003). Pluralistic ignorance and hooking up. *Journal of Sex Research,* 40, 129–133.

18 Harris, K. M. (2009). The National Longitudinal Study of Adolescent Health (Add Health). Chapel Hill, NC: Carolina Population Center, University of North Carolina at Chapel Hill.

19 Hinlicky, Sarah E., (1998, October). Subversive virginity. *First Things.* Retrieved from http://www.firstthings.com/article/2009/03/002-subversive-virginity-3.

CHAPTER 7

1   Regnerus, M., & Uecker, J. (2011). *Premarital sex in America: How you Americans meet, mate, and think about marrying.* New York: Oxford University Press.

2   Moran, J. (1995). *The erotic mind: Unlocking the inner sources of passion and fulfillment.* New York: HarperCollins.

3   Murray, B., & Fortinberry, A. (2004). *Creating optimism: A proven 7-step program for overcoming depression.* New York: McGraw-Hill.

4   Reuters. (2011). Not all young Australian men want more sex: Survey. *Reuters.* Retrieved from http://www.reuters.com/article/2011/05/02/us-sex-survey-idUSTRE7414SI20110502.

5   Harris, K. M. (2009). The National Longitudinal Study of Adolescent Health (Add Health). Chapel Hill, NC: Carolina Population Center, University of North Carolina at Chapel Hill.

6   Meston, C. M., & Buss, D. M. (2009). *Why women have sex: Understanding sexual motivations from adventure to revenge (and everything in between).* New York: Henry Holt.

7   Crawford, M., & Popp, D. (2003). Sexual double standards: A review and methodological critique of two decades of research. *Journal of Sex Research, 40,* 13–26.

8   Laumann, E. O., Gagnon, J. H., Michael, R. T., & Michaels, S. (1994). *The social organization of sexuality: Sexual practices in the United States.* Chicago: University of Chicago Press.

9   Campbell, A. (2008). The morning after the night before: Affective reactions to one-night stands among mated and unmated women and men. *Human Nature, 19,* 157–173.

CHAPTER 8

1   Mickelson, K. D., Kessler, R. C., Shaver, P. R. (1997). Adult attachment in a nationally representative sample. *Journal of Personality and Social Psychology, 73*(5), 1092–1106.

2   Etxebarria, I., Ortiz, M. J., Conejero, S., & Pascual, A. (2009). Intensity of habitual guilt in men and women: Differences in interpersonal sensitivity and the tendency towards anxious-aggressive guilt. *Spanish Journal of Psychology, 12*(2), 540–554.

3   Levant, R. F. (2001). Desperately seeking language: Understanding, assessing and treating normative male alexithymia. In G. R. Brooks

and G. Good (Eds.). *The new handbook of counseling and psychotherapy for men.* (Vol. 1, pp. 424–443). San Francisco: Jossey-Bass.

4   Jung, C. G. (1938). *Psychology and religion.* New Haven, CT: Yale University Press.

5   University of Michigan. (2010). Predicting divorce: Study shows how fight styles affect marriage. *ScienceDaily.* Retrieved from http://www.sciencedaily.com/releases/2010/09/100928152022.htm.

6   University of Michigan. (2008). A good fight may keep you and your marriage healthy. *ScienceDaily.* Retrieved from http://www.sciencedaily.com/releases/2008/01/080122173036.htm.

7   Algoe, S. B., Gable, S. L., & Maisel, N. C. (2010). It's the little things: Everyday gratitude as a booster shot for romantic relationships. *Personal Relationships,* 17(2), 217–233.

8   UCLA. (2012). Here is what real commitment to your marriage means. *ScienceDaily.* Retrieved from http://www.sciencedaily.com/releases/2012/02/120201181453.htm.

9   Jay, M. (2012). *The defining decade: Why your twenties matter—and how to make the most of them now.* New York: Hachette Book Group.

CHAPTER 9

1   Petrou, A. (2011). Internet plays Cupid for the older generation. *TechEye.* Retrieved from http://www.techeye.net/internet/internet-plays-cupid-for-the-older-generation.

2   Personal interview. Josh Meyers, CEO, PeopleMedia.com.

3   University of Missouri at Columbia. (2010). The joy is in the social hunt: Facebook users more engaged emotionally when conducting specific searches. *ScienceDaily.* Retrieved from http://www.sciencedaily.com/releases/2010/04/100423113735.htm.

4   American Sociological Association. (2010). Internet access at home increases the likelihood that adults will be in relationships, study finds. *ScienceDaily.* Retrieved from http://www.sciencedaily.com/releases/2010/08/100816095615.htm.

5   Smith, A. (2011). How Americans use text messaging. *Pew Internet.* Retrieved from http://pewinternet.org/Reports/2011/Cell-Phone-Texting-2011/Main-Report.aspx.

6   Linden, D. J. (2011). Food, pleasure, and evolution. *Psychology Today.* Retrieved from http://www.psychologytoday.com/blog/the-compass-pleasure/201103/food-pleasure-and-evolution.

7   Rudder, C. (2010). The biggest lies people tell online. *OkTrends*.
     Retrieved from http://blog.okcupid.com/index.php/the-biggest-lies-in-
     online-dating.

8   University of Montreal. (2009). Are the effects of pornography
     negligible? *ScienceDaily*. Retrieved from http://www.sciencedaily.
     com/releases/2009/12/091201111202.htm.

9   Rutgers University. (2011). Psychologists link election wins with
     higher Internet porn use. *ScienceDaily*. Retrieved from http://
     www.sciencedaily.com/releases/2011/04/110419111431.htm.

10   Regnerus, M., & Uecker, J. (2011). *Premarital sex in America: How
     you Americans meet, mate, and think about marrying*. New York:
     Oxford University Press.

11   Weiss, R. (2012). What's up with porn? *Psych Central*. Retrieved from
     http://blogs.psychcentral.com/sex/2012/02/what%e2%80%99s-up-
     with-porn.

12   Weiss, R. (2012). Sexual dysfunction: The escalating price of abusing
     porn. *Psych Central*. Retrieved from http://blogs.psychcentral.com/
     sex/2012/05/abusing-porn.

13   Weiss, R. (2012). How much porn is too much porn? *Psych Central*.
     Retrieved from http://blogs.psychcentral.com/sex/2012/03/porn.

14   Weiss. (2012). What's up with porn? *Psych Central*.

CHAPTER 10

1   Hollander, D. (1997). *101 lies men tell women*. New York: Harper
     Perennial.

2   Duke University. (2007). When to have a child? A new approach to
     the decision. *ScienceDaily*. Retrieved from http://www.sciencedaily.
     com/releases/2007/11/071107160144.htm.

3   Sefcek, J. A., Brumbach, B. H., Vásquez, G., & Miller, G. F. (2006).
     The evolutionary psychology of human mate choice: How ecology,
     genes, fertility, and fashion influence our mating behavior. In M. R.
     Kauth (Ed.). *On the Evolution of Sexual Attraction [Special Issue]*.
     Journal of Psychology & Human Sexuality, 18(2/3), 125–182.

4   Mickelson, K. D., Kessler, R. C., & Shaver, P. R. (1997). Adult
     attachment in a nationally representative sample. *Journal of
     Personality and Social Psychology*, 73(5), 1092–1106.

5   Platek, S. M., & Shackelford, T. K. (2006). *Female infidelity and
     paternal uncertainty: Evolutionary perspectives on male anti-
     cuckoldry tactics*. Cambridge, UK: Cambridge University Press.

Index

Attachment strategy, in love
    detox, 50, 60, 67
Attachment style, 50, 60, 94,
    131
  electronic communication
    and, 206–7
  for forming relationship
    life plan, 91, 94, 95, 96
  secure vs. insecure, 61–63,
    67, 76, 91, 95
  sexual strategies linked
    with, 73, 76
Attention, male
  during love detox, 156, 157
  power equated with, 154,
    155
  replacements for, 160
  types of men providing,
    152–53
  women seeking, 150, 151
Autism, 19, 21
Avoidance. *See* Attachment-
    related avoidance;
    Emotional avoidance

B

Backup men, of single
    women, 150–53, 210
Bad boys
  arousal from, 156
  attraction to, 70, 123–26
  five signs of, <u>121</u>
  success formula of, 125
Birth(s)
  out-of-wedlock, 8, 11, <u>23</u>
  premature, of humans,
    32–33
Blended families, 38, 101,
    102

Body odor, immune system
    and, 30–31
Bonding
  with children, 49
  desire for, 25, 166
  improving chances of, 138
  purpose of, 7, 61
Bonding hormone. *See*
    Oxytocin
Boundaries
  in early relationships,
    188
  setting, 178, 191, 205,
    216
  with shame tolerance,
    179–80
  violation of, 151
Bradbury, Thomas, 187
Brain
  attachment injuries and,
    34
  love affecting, 40–41,
    55–56
  motherhood and, 29
  rewiring, 71, 197, 209
Breadwinners, female, 9–10,
    <u>10</u>, 37, 38, 39, 58, 107
Busby, Dean, 133, 136–37,
    149
Buss, David, 43, 136, 164,
    209

C

Cannold, Leslie, 20
Care, giving and receiving,
    176–77
Career advancement, of
    women, 12, 78, 79, 84,
    151

H

Haselton, Martie G., 43, 136
"Having it all" myth, 84–85, 221
Health
  emotional, 166–67, 190
  marriage benefiting, 104, 122
Heartbreak, 8, 44, 104, 123, 149, 217
Herpes, genital, 46, 47
Hierarchy of human needs, 135
High-supply sexual economy, 4, 108, 198
  creating healthy relationship in, 216
  leaving, 137–38, 144, 146–47
  male dissatisfaction with, 161
  marriage in, 115, 142
  negative effects of
    on family, 11, 39, 104
    on women, 56, 131, 134
  technology use in, 206–7
  women's reasons for joining, 25, 56, 72
HIV, 46, 47
Hollander, Dory, 43
Homemakers
  female, 79, <u>81</u>
  male, 79, 105–6, 107, 111
Hookups
  addiction to, 4
  attachment insecurity leading to, 62, 67, 70
  dangers of, 9, 10, 39, 44, 47

female misconceptions about, 43, 135, 136
  men and, 43
  myth about, 44–45, 132–33
  reasons for choosing, 25, 39, 43
  short-term sexual strategies in, 77
Hrdy, Sarah Blaffer, 34
Humor, in healthy fighting, 185
Hunger Games, The, 35
Hunter-gatherer ancestors
  bonding of, 61
  cheating affecting, 118
  cravings inherited from, 197–98
  mate selection by, 25
  sexual risks of, 45
Hunter-gatherer society
  access to women in, 14
  division of labor in, 34–35
  human behavior influenced by, 31
  monogamy in, 33, 42–43
  successful women in, 26, 27, 32
  traditional family in, 33–34
  work and leisure in, 35–36
Hunters
  female attraction to, 107–8
  in online dating, 201
  women as, 35
Hymowitz, Kay, 15, 19

I

Immune system, body odor and, 30–31

Relationships *(cont.)*
  healthy *(cont.)*
    role of sex in, 188–90
    technology in, 193, 196
    traits of, 157, 176, 186,
      188, 212–13
  influences on, 61, 137
  junk food analogy about,
    198
  long-term
    care in, 176
    conflict resolution in,
      183
    courting behavior in, 128
    delayed sex and, 149
    disinterest in, 62, <u>75</u>, 95
    female-friendly locale
      for, 165
    obstacles to, 219
    women desiring, 68, 95
  romantic, 71, 104, 114, 195
  romantic vs. rational love
    in, 59
  sexual promiscuity and, 77
  short-term
    addiction to, 159
    attitude leading to,
      217–18
    avoiding friends seeking,
      164
    bad boys and, <u>121</u>
    choice in, 157
    negative effects of, 77,
      166, 190, 219–20
    when to have, 95, 166
  stay-over, 101–2
  technology in *(see*
    Technology, in
    relationships)
  types to consider, 39–40

Relationship system,
    establishing, 187–91
Religion
  as predictor of monogamy,
    119
  in relationship life plan,
    93–94, 96
Reproduction goals, in
    relationship life plan,
    93
*Reshaping the Work-Family
  Debate,* 7, 79
Rewards, random, addiction
    from, 124–26
Richer Sex, The, 9, 59
Richters, Juliet, 162, 188
Romantic love
  definition of, 41–42
  oppressive effects of, 58
  perfection during, 180–81
  rational love vs., 58–59,
    186–87
Romantic relationships
  healing from, 71
  health benefits of, 104
  men valuing, 114
  technology and, 195

S

Sahlins, Marshall, 36
Saying "No" to sex
  benefits of, 155, 156
  conviction for, 147–48
  strategies for, 139, <u>142</u>,
    143–44
  token "No" when, 144–45
  understanding, <u>145</u>
  women's difficulty with,
    141–42

V

Vasopressin, love increasing,
41
Vibrators, 160
Victorian England,
prostitution in, 13–14
Virginity, 72, 132, 146–49

W

Wealth
attraction to, 107
of cougars, 18
of long-term couples, 10
marriage and, 38, 100
mate selection affecting, 49
as predictor of cheating,
120
Wedding planners, women
as, 87
What, No Baby?, 20
When Harry Met Sally, 151
Why Women Have Sex, 164
Williams, Joan, 7, 79, 84
Wilson, Sarah Hinlicky,
146–47

Y

Yagan, Sam, 197, 199–200,
201–2, <u>212</u>